DISCARD

Rewarding Work

Rewarding Work

■ ■ ■

*How to Restore Participation
and Self-Support to Free Enterprise*

EDMUND S. PHELPS

Harvard University Press
Cambridge, Massachusetts
London, England
1997

Library of Congress Cataloging-in-Publication Data

Phelps, Edmund S.
    Rewarding work : how to restore participation and self-support to
free enterprise / Edmund S. Phelps
        p. cm.
Includes bibliographical references and index.
ISBN 0-674-09495-6 (alk. paper)
    1. Employment subsidies—United States. I. Title.
    HC110.S9P47 1997
    331.2'16—dc21   96-50204

To *Viviana Montdor Phelps,*

my wife

Preface

In one of the dark days of the 1970s it struck me that little recovery from the social ills in America can be expected when the pay available to the less talented and less privileged in the marketplace is so low as to leave them unintegrated with society and incapable of doing anything with their lives. Yet scrapping free enterprise for a system of socialist make-work was the last thing we—or they—wanted.

The immediate and reliable way out, I felt, was some kind of subsidy or tax credit designed to pull up the abysmally low rewards to work. I tried to sound this theme in the 1980s (in my textbook, *Political Economy,* for example). But few listened. Evidently an in-depth development of the idea was needed.

I found the opportunity to develop a concrete scheme for presentation at a 1990 conference on poverty at the Jerome Levy Institute of Bard College. Its positive effects on low wage rates were clear. It took more time, though, to understand its effects on unemployment. Finally I saw that a suitably designed scheme would be double-barreled, reducing unemployment of low-wage workers and boosting paychecks at the same time. This time around my efforts were bombarded with objections and opposed out of long attachment to other approaches and perspectives.

This book is an attempt to make the required case. I set forth the argument for low-wage employment subsidies as systematically and plainly as I can so that it can be evaluated by the general public and, if all goes well, considered for enactment into law.

I hasten to add that over these years there were parallel lines of thought being taken by others, though I was unaware of them at the time. In this country, Daniel Hammermesh, Robert Haveman,

James Palmer, and John Pencavel did pioneering work in the early 1980s. In Britain, Richard Layard led a team in the mid-1980s. In the present decade, a variant of the idea has been championed in Europe by Dennis Snower.

This project has received financial support from several sources over the years as I struggled to gain the necessary background of facts and findings and to grasp the wide range of issues raised by the proposal. The Russell Sage Foundation appointed me a visiting scholar in 1992–93. Subsequently the Bradley Foundation provided a two-year research grant to further this project. The John M. Olin Foundation awarded a book grant to help with preparation of the manuscript.

One of the literatures this book draws on is my bread and butter—economics—and the discussion here reflects my own past work. For example, the framework takes off from the concept of the natural unemployment rate, which I helped to originate decades ago—though mine is a natural rate that moves around and that mankind can reduce. My recent research on the unemployment and wages of low-wage workers has been particularly useful, and I want to acknowledge my very great debt to two young economists, both former students of mine, who have been wonderful co-workers in that research, Hian Teck Hoon, National University of Singapore, and Gylfi Zoega, Birkbeck College, University of London.

I also want to thank Michael Aronson and Camille Smith of Harvard University Press for their commitment and contributions to this project.

Contents

■

Prologue

As recently as our Bicentennial the values we associated with the Republic were still those of liberty and independence—of enterprise and self-reliance. The Founders had cleared the ground for market capitalism. Labor and capital were to be free of the state, not obliged to curry favor with the government for a job or for permission to start or close an enterprise. The Founders also thought it wise to make the livelihood of productive persons depend on their own efforts, without a free ride from the state. It was believed that the opportunity and incentive offered by this system would best encourage the creativity and self-development that are essential to happiness.

The expectation was that, thus liberated and motivated, able-bodied and competent men and women would be capable of finding work and earning their own way. And they would have enough not only to sustain themselves but to participate in social life—to take on family and civic responsibilities and to share to a degree the ways of the community. This was the American experiment: to try the new system of private enterprise and self-help in the hope it would meet the requirements of economic inclusion and social cohesion.

For most of its ensuing history this system was an earthly paradise in which people, through their work, supported themselves, developed their talents, and took part in the community. It

1

helped that, in its first century, America was still mostly rural.[1] Labor was so scarce that all hands were of considerable value in gaining a foothold on the new land.[2] Access to community activities and discourse was easy. It was Tocqueville's Democratic America.[3] In the second century urbanization and immigration threatened cohesion, though Henry Ford's assembly line idea arrived in 1914 to revive the returns to physical labor. Discrimination was a barrier to inclusion for many, though it was finally countered with legislation in the 1960s. Other countries carried out this American experiment, as we often call it, but none more intently and more successfully than ours. If that success has been exaggerated to mythic proportions, it is still an image we measure our country against.

By the 1970s, though, there were signs of trouble in paradise. In the nation's cities an alternative economy was surfacing of street vendors, panhandlers, hustlers, and drug dealers. An array of social pathologies—crime, drug abuse, and illegitimacy—became conspicuous in the poorer urban areas. Since then, several indicators have worsened. Homelessness became a national phenomenon in the 1980s. Gang violence and violent crimes by youth have soared in the 1990s. The perceived safety of person and property has further declined. Relations between ethnic groups and economic classes have frayed. Throughout this long span the level of dependency increased enormously. Gainful employment among the disadvantaged, in particular among low-wage men, declined dramatically. About twice as many of them do not participate in the labor force in the 1990s as in the early 1970s, and of those in the labor force, about twice as many are unemployed now than then.[4] Large numbers fell back on the entitlement programs of the welfare system. The rising caseload of qualifying clients caused social assistance outlays to rise relative to national income by one-third from 1974 to 1994 and the outlay per worker to rise by one-half.[5] Many others, especially men with little earning power, turned to illegal activity. A million and a half men are now in prison or jail.

In its third century, then, the American experiment has ceased to deliver the inclusion and cohesion it did in the past. With this failure has come a serious decline in civic responsibility and social organization among the economically disadvantaged members of the working-age population. Adapting to these setbacks, the American system has mutated toward welfare capitalism.

This social breakdown and unrest, I argue, can be traced to economic forces that have deprived a great many less advantaged workers of much of the power of their labor. It is apparent from observation of poor areas that many working-age people can no longer be self-sustaining; they need assistance with their food, housing, and medical care to get by. Others can survive but cannot earn a decent living—cannot afford out of their wages the basic things people generally want to do in their lives, such as raising a child or two. Still others find enough support from welfare or crime that they see no gain from a job.

If reduced earning power is the prime mover in the story, there is a paradox. Wages—after adjusting for inflation—are considerably higher in all strata of the labor force today than in the 1950s, let alone, say, the 1920s. Why, then, the social problems of the past twenty years after so many decades of social gains? The answer lies in the profound shifts in the structure of opportunities and resources in America: the long downhill slide in the wages available to those in the lower reaches of the wage scale *relative* to the opportunities of others and to the other sources of support they can draw on.

Low-wage men began slowly to fall further behind the rest of the labor force as early as the 1950s. The decline in their relative earning power (in their wage relative to the median wage) gathered speed over the next two decades, reaching 9 percent in the 1970s.[6] By the end of the decade the wage gap was too wide for these workers to afford even the semblance of a working-class lifestyle, let alone a middle-class lifestyle. This relative decline, moreover, occurred against the backdrop of an upward trend in the relative wage of women at all wage levels, so more and more low-wage women found it possible to make ends meet without a male breadwinner. And with the expansions of the welfare state in the 1960s women no longer needed a husband to raise children and far fewer elderly needed to depend on their children's earning power for their support. Thus men were deprived of certain central roles that most wage earners in their fathers' generation had filled. In that sense, their work was devalued.

The 1980s ushered in a new phase in which, while their relative wage went on declining not much faster than before, that relative decline meant an absolute fall in the wage of low-paid men, since the median wage was no longer rising—it was, in fact, falling somewhat. The steep fall in the wage of low-paid men, when there was no force acting to shrink their cushion of nonwage resources and other options, weakened their motivation as employees. That in turn raised their costs to employers, reducing their employability and causing their unemployment rate to rise to a new level.

The welfare system was a contributing factor here. When deep cuts in pay were required to preserve enterprises, the open-ended system of entitlements at fixed levels of benefits offered substantial nonwage resources that were impervious to the fall of wages. This magnified the effects of the reduced rewards to work on participation and unemployment.

The effect of the abysmal earning power of the disadvantaged has now metastasized beyond low income and high unemployment. The deprivation and idleness have created a sense of exclusion. The inability to earn much more than what family, charity, and the welfare system can provide has created a feeling of powerlessness. There is despair that the future will hold any possibility of personal development. This outlook undoubtedly plays a part in the rise of alcoholism, drug addiction, and a propensity to violence.

As a result, the massive economic disadvantage now prevailing in our country presents a serious cost and threat to the rest of society. It is the main source of the social pathologies attacking and weakening our cities. It is the cause, not the effect, of the much-decried culture of poverty and the decline of morality. These social effects make prevailing economic disadvantage a problem for all of society, not just for the disadvantaged themselves.

What to do? Obviously the safety net of social assistance and social insurance does not cure the social ills rooted in inadequate wages.

One political party aims to kick away the props of social assistance and some social insurance programs in order to push the beneficiaries and their communities back to work. But that would not raise their inadequate wage rates either. So most of those driven into the labor market would find their wages, as before, too meager to provide self-support and to restore their social cohesion. The other party champions increases in the statutory minimum wage. Such steps increase low-end wages. But they do not achieve the much-needed reintegration of low-wage persons into the world of jobs and business. We need to foster *both* inclusion and cohesion while preserving capitalism and reclaiming self-reliance in the bargain.

To raise future wages by raising future productivity, the one party presses for lower tax rates on the belief that faster economic growth will improve the rewards of everyone, especially the disadvantaged, at least in the long run. The other party champions increased subsidies to encourage young people to choose more schooling. But these futuristic visions will do little to reclaim the value of work and self-support *now*—within a very few years.

Fortunately, a remedy exists. We *can* reverse the critical decline of wages and employment among the disadvantaged in this country. Poor communities can be raised up as surely as the decline of pay and jobs has beaten them down. The method is not any of the instruments in current use.

The method is the introduction of employment subsidies. In the version I advocate, they take the form of continuing tax credits to private enterprises for their continuing employment of low-wage workers. The subsidy plan rewards the firm for as many workers as it employs. The system of subsidies is targeted at workers whose private productivity is low (as evidenced by the low hourly labor cost that firms are willing to incur for their services), since it is these workers whose inclusion in the capitalist economy and cohesion with the mainstream of society are weak and whose social responsibility is undermined when they are paid a wage to match their low productivity.

The beauty of this method is that it operates to drive both the wages and the unemployment rates of low-wage workers in the desired direction. The subsidies induce firms to hire more low-wage workers, pulling their employment up, their unemployment down. Wages then rise, as firms seek to restore employee incentives, until they finally match the increased wage that firms can afford to pay, thanks to the subsidies. The subsidies deliver both improved social cohesion and increased economic inclusion.

Understandably, this proposal raises questions. What is so valuable about working and earning? (Why not just provide people with a stake of money—like the economists' demogrant, or "negative income tax"?) After two centuries of economic advance, how can there be extensive poverty, and more poverty than a half-century ago? What harm does the position of workers with low earning power do to the rest of society? What assurance is there that the subsidy plan, targeted on the lowest paid, would improve their economic opportunities? How would it affect the working class, who would receive little or no subsidy money? What would an adequate subsidy plan cost the government, and what would be the budgetary savings and revenue gains? Would the subsidies require a sizable tax increase, at least for a while? What could justify even a temporary tax increase to help low-wage workers when there are so many others in our society and overseas who are even poorer? Wouldn't the employment subsidies dampen workers' incentives to seek increased education? If so, wouldn't such a side effect make them unacceptable?

The chapters of this book are devoted to answering these questions and more. As I see it, the answers are good enough. It is necessary to view the matter in perspective. Employment subsidies are not a perfect instrument. Society will not be improved in every aspect. There will still be some place for social assistance and major roles for public education and public measures to foster economic growth. With the introduction of employment subsidies some of these older instruments will be needed more than ever, others less. But these traditional measures cannot deliver reliably and quickly the boost to wages and employment among the low-paid that must underpin the solution to the social problems of recent decades. Low-wage employment subsidies, their imperfections notwithstanding, are the most effective instrument we have available to re-create lost opportunities for work and self-support, to restore inclusion and cohesion, and to reclaim responsibility for oneself and others.

The Problem

▪

1

.

Why Work?

Work is at the center of a normal life. Most people who have experienced a job cannot get along without its important rewards.

One of the most important rewards in most jobs is mental stimulation. They present a continual series of exercises in problem-solving: figuring out how to do new tasks well or old tasks better, solving difficulties with colleagues, and calculating how to win better terms. Of course mastering the simplest jobs will generally be less of a learning experience than a career in the most complex and demanding jobs. Jobs do not all have to provide a mental workout, though, to sustain the main point. It is enough to contrast the interestingness of jobs with the terrible aimlessness and boredom that come with not having one. The reflections of people in humble lines of work show that they learn much from their work and from its school of hard knocks.[1]

Thorstein Veblen, America's first prominent economist—following hints from the great psychologist William James—built on his version of this point a century ago: there is more to mankind's drives than hedonism and the propensity to "truck and barter." There is a drive for improvement and a curiosity about how things work or can be made to work better—the "instinct of workmanship."[2] Some social reformers, such as the philosopher John Dewey, voiced the hope that industrialists could offer workplaces in which the workers would solve problems together. Let workers build the whole shoe and the whole ship rather than be confined to one repetitive operation.[3]

Veblen went on to argue that this instinct had been discouraged by the rise of the commercial economy run by financiers, who cared only for the bottom line, and suppressed entirely with the arrival of the industrial economy. Today economists say that an industrialist is glad to make the workplace more engaging and more participatory, even in the range where further moves in that direction will raise costs of production, as long as there are workers who in return for the resulting job satisfactions will accept the reduced wage the industrialist may be obliged to offer. Now, offices and factories have become generally smaller and more participatory for middle- and high-income workers—General Motors' Saturn plant being the best-known example. But relatively low-paid workers feel they cannot afford to accept the lower wage needed to buy basic job satisfactions—not in their present circumstances.

Another benefit of work is that it fulfills the desire to have a place in society—a calling, in bygone language. Many people feel a need to contribute. And many feel a need to belong, which means to be depended on (instead of always depending on)—even if only for small things and by a small group. As the responsibilities and challenges of a job are met a person's self-confidence grows and, with it, the ability to meet other demands. A lone individual can set goals for himself and grow more able, as Defoe's fictional Crusoe did, but responsibilities and unimagined challenges have to come from others.

These two functions of work, intellectual and social, were apparently what the British economist Alfred Marshall had in mind when, toward the close of the last century, he wrote:

The business by which a person earns his livelihood generally fills his thoughts during by far the greater part of those hours in which his mind is at its best; during them his character is being formed by the way in which he uses his faculties, by the thoughts and feelings it suggests, and by his relations to his associates in work.[4]

Our jobs become a central part of who we are.

Yet another benefit of work is a relatively recent discovery. The lack or loss of a job may be dangerous to your health. A Paris physician, reflecting on a long practice, reported that an extraordinary number of his patients died within a year or two of their retirement. The physician's explanation was that their mental and physical health depended on a degree of order and routine in their lives.[5] There is a sort of ritual about going to work. Jobs lend a rhythm to daily life for people farming the land and those in nine-to-five jobs as well. Self-employed persons simulate this order through self-imposed deadlines and compulsive habits. The most successful writers and composers develop regimens to follow as if their lives depended on it.

Work also has material rewards, of course, and these are of the utmost importance. Even people with independent incomes do not find it easy to pass up the material gain from working. The downward trend in hours worked stopped at the end of the 1940s. Since then, the average workweek in manufacturing has changed little, fluctuating around 41 hours, and the workweek in most other industries has been similarly stable (falling in retail trade and rising in mining). It might be wondered why, with present-day wage levels so far above those a century or even a half-century ago, anyone would want to work more than a few hours a week for the income.

There are compelling reasons for wanting the earnings of a rather long workday. First, the very young aside, people need income to pay for leisure activities. The abundance of leisure provided by a half-time job would be, for most, unaffordable without transfusions of funds from family, spouse, or the welfare state. The length of the full-time workweek represents a balance between income and leisure. Second, the increase in longevity means that a given lifetime of earned income is now stretched thin and is therefore all the more important to have.[6]

Furthermore, income is wanted not only for one's own consumption and saving but for others. One wants to provide for children and families in order to play the role of parent and spouse. Finally, people's choices between income and leisure, hence the "needs" we infer they have, are very much influenced by social conventions and relationships. It might be possible to function in a company on a 30-hour workweek, but very few employees would be accepted on that basis when everyone else in the company is on a 40-hour week. Furthermore, a decision to earn radically less would involve a loss of social contacts, as well as a loss of consumption. Many of a person's satisfactions come from being able to share the experiences of others, and this requires having an adequate income relative to the others.

These material rewards from work become of huge importance when they are large enough to enable one to be self-supporting— to earn by one's own efforts the opportunity to enjoy the basic comforts, to have a family, and to share to a degree in the life of the community. Few circumstances undermine a person's self-esteem more than dependency on others for such material support. The last step in our entrance to adulthood is the demonstration that we can stand free of our parents by landing a job paying a living wage, and the first step on leaving responsible adulthood is to surrender the making of decisions regarding investments and expenditure to grown children or surrogates. Furthermore, when we become dependent upon others or upon the state, we are apt to have much less choice about purchases than when we are on our own. Parents offer income in kind, not a check with no strings attached, and social welfare agencies provide housing, food stamps, medical care, and so forth, but not much cash.

The value put on self-support—on economic independence— and on participation in society's productive activity is now recognized as nearly universal. These desires are evidently as natural to women as to men. In his studies of black American communities the sociologist William Julius Wilson has emphasized the anchor that steady work and decent pay used to provide for black men and the families they supported. "Work organizes life," as Wilson puts it. Oxfam's Food for Work program in East Africa demonstrated the considerable satisfaction that women in poor areas found in growing their own food and thus to a degree earning their own living.

When many residents of a community are unable to find work at a wage high enough to support themselves and their families, not only those individuals and families but the functioning of the entire community may be impaired. As failure becomes the pattern in a community, its young people will not acquire the ambition and optimism that a community already integrated into the national economy needs to avoid disintegration and that a developing community must have to become integrated. A sociologist teaching a largely Muslim student body in Marseille, Leila Yehiawi, sees her students as doomed to be "second-class citizens to whom France is inaccessible" by the deprivation and idleness around them. "Work is the backbone of integration," she concludes.[7]

In a society as individualistic as ours, in which making it—gaining some measure of success and achievement—counts for so much, this exclusion from a rewarding place in the economy's mainstream is particularly painful. And this marginalization is even more damaging where, as in American society, the main national purpose is to protect and advance an economic system, a system designed for the mutual advantage of citizens in the pursuit of wealth and personal growth. "The business of America," as Calvin Coolidge said, "is business."

Fortunately, there is a way to restore opportunities for work in the mainstream and, in doing so, to renew the possibility of economic independence and to stimulate economic integration.

2

.

America's Second-Class Workers

Advocates of *laissez-faire*—the free-market species of free enter-prise—suppose that in a free-market economy the competition of enterprises for employees and the quest of workers for the best opportunities provide all workers with gainful employment and with wages on which they can support themselves and their fami-lies. That some have far less desirable jobs than the rest is not a concern of society, since everyone has the resources to pursue his or her own self-development.

The premise of this doctrine—the value of self-realization and independence—receives a more sympathetic hearing today than it once did. Antipathy toward the rich or the super-rich, as if they were hereditary barons owning all the land (and land was every-thing), is no longer intense. Few consider it wrong that finalists take most of the prize money at the big tennis championships. Likewise, few see it as undesirable that among those betting large sums on commercial ventures or market developments the lion's share of the returns go to those who are unusually talented or lucky or both. One reason is that these competitions are open to all—even if some who might have been good at them did not receive the prerequisites of language, education, or encouragement when they were young. Another reason is that these competitions, with their outsize rewards, do not damage others. It's not like a shootout that injures bystanders who don't join in. There is no

16

kind of compensation, no indemnity, needing to be paid. A character in Shakespeare's *As You Like It* expresses this outlook:

> I am a true labourer: I earn that I eat, get what I wear, owe no man hate, envy no man's happiness, glad of other men's good.

There is a pragmatic consideration too. We all gain from a system that offers large payoffs to successful entrepreneurship and speculation. The instruments of taxation give society a second chance to spread the income around, but, as a great many citizens understand, at some point levying a still higher tax rate on those rewards would dampen investment and speculation by so much that the total tax revenue received would actually be reduced. Even if there were no such incentive effects of increased tax rates, inequality at the top is hardly *the*—or even *a*—big social problem. If we could siphon off one-third, say, of the excess of the wage income of those in the top tenth (currently around $85,000 per head annually) over the wage income in the next-to-top tenth (currently around $40,000 per head annually) and we distributed it to the remaining workers, each in proportion to his or her wage, their wages would rise by only about 11 percent. All in all, therefore, it appears to be a mistake to rail against inequality at the top. (Inequality at the bottom, however, is quite different, as it may, if pronounced enough, effectively threaten people's economic independence and inclusion in society's functioning.)

What the rosy view taken by laissez-faire leaves out is the problem of meager wages. Laissez-faire doctrine assumes each person is either amply productive and hence capable of self-support *or* wholly unproductive and hence incapable of self-help. All those of the first type are workers and counted on to provide for themselves; all of the second type are nonworkers and candidates for charity and public aid.

The economy today clearly has another category, a class of workers whose employment and wage prospects are too poor to support a lifestyle remotely approaching that of the middle class. The middle class can afford out of their earnings several basic goods that define their lifestyle: rudimentary health care, the responsibilities of marriage, raising one or two children and sending them to college, participation in community affairs, hobbies, travel, and insurance to retire at the accustomed level when old or disabled. (The working class may have to omit a few of these goods or settle for downscaled versions. The upper class differ mainly in quantitative terms: they are able to marry many times, support many children, and retire or semi-retire relatively early.) The less fortunate cannot expect to do many of these things, if any at all. A few will win a lottery, but that will not be a typical experience.

All the members of this second class of workers may be said to suffer one or more disadvantages in the contest for earnings. Some suffer natural disadvantages—a deficiency in natural attributes such as stamina and reaction time or some mismatch between attribute and the required tasks.[1] Some suffer social disadvantages—an underprivileged family background or school environment resulting in deficiencies in basic skills or attitudes and racial or ethnic prejudice leading to discrimination in hiring and wage-setting.[2] It is implausible to think that social background and prejudices subject whole communities to below-subsistence earning power. But these social factors could obviously make the difference between self-sufficiency and dependency for workers who start off with a sizable natural disadvantage. In the catalog of the disadvantaged are also those who, though they may not have been disadvantaged at the outset, were unlucky in their choice of a career or region. There is only a difference of degree, after all, between a lifelong disadvantage and an equal misfortune that starts in mid-life. The term "disadvantaged" seems suitable enough to label the category of workers faced with earnings opportunities that effectively exclude them from significant aspects of middle-class life.

Where Serious Disadvantage Starts

How low does a worker's wage have to be to put a middle-class life out of reach? Some arbitrariness is inherent in the answer. (Is the test a deprivation of some really big thing, like marrying, or of some not quite so big thing, like a four-college for one's child instead of a two-year college?) And the dividing line in terms of the hourly pay rate will differ from worker to worker, since they vary in the overtime and multiple jobs they can handle and in the risk of being laid off. (For one worker a $5 hourly wage might mean $9,000 a year, for another it might be only $6,000, while for a veritable workhorse it might amount to $15,000.) For purposes of discussion we may think of those individuals working the full-time workweek (about 40 hours) 50 weeks a year, without likely spells of unemployment to worry about. (Obviously those in part-time jobs or having frequent spells of unemployment must have a much higher hourly wage rate to do as well.)

Think of the middle class as those occupying the low part of the upper half of the earnings distribution, and the working class as those occupying the high part of the lower half of the distribution. (The working class is a Britishism, but a helpful distinction.) Then the median wage earners—the ones exactly in the middle—are at the bottom of the middle class. In 1995 the median wage earner in the private sector earned about $10 per hour. Working at that hourly rate for a full-time workweek of 40 hours would yield $400 a week and, with no spells of unemployment, around $20,000 annually. The median family, having 1.6 such earners, would thus have annual earnings of about $32,000—somewhat less if one or both worked part-time hours. (In fact, median family income is higher, as it includes nonwage income from assets accumulated for retirement, but wages—so-called earned income—are a better measure of the consumption level that is sustainable over the whole life.) Although these figures may strike us as low, they indicate a huge gap between the middle class and the low wage earners in the American economy.

Compare the workers at the low end: those whose wage is only the statutory minimum wage—still $4.70 an hour at this writing. Clearly it is impossible to finance anything resembling a middle-class lifestyle on that wage rate, which in annual terms is some $9,400 per year for full-time work. Everyone has a picture of the life of workers receiving wages somewhat below the statutory minimum wage. Most of them are migrant workers working on minimum-wage-exempt farms or urban workers, many of them immigrants, in illegal sweatshops; they clearly fall into the "second-class" group. So, just as clearly, do the appreciable number of workers with wage rates tightly bunched at the minimum wage or a little above it.

Equally clearly, a wage of $6 an hour does not catapult those earning it into the middle class. And yet this is the top wage in the bottom fifth—the wage of the worker standing at the twentieth percentile of the distribution. It does not seem at all likely that an hourly wage of a dollar more will be sufficient either. A wage of $7 per hour, or, working full time, $14,000 per year, does not afford some rather important purchases that would be possible with the lower-middle-class wage of $10 per hour. Such workers have to do without owning their home or sending a child to college or traveling or some combination of those in order to afford things of higher priority.

Are these workers really poor? There is no denying that regularly working full-time jobholders have access to a range of goods that would have been the envy of the majority of workers a half-century ago. Many observers therefore wonder whether the relatively low earnings of today's disadvantaged any longer mean "poverty" in the standard sense of the term. The income of workers one-tenth of the way up the scale (those in the tenth percentile) is now about the same as the income—expressed in today's dollars to allow for the inflation between then and now—of the *median* worker in 1955, and we do not think of the latter as poor. But the ability of most of the disadvantaged to obtain, one way or another, the goods that are essential to existence and even to own luxuries such as a car or a television set does not mean that their situation does not exact a heavy toll on them. The disadvantaged bear burdens not revealed by standard measures of income and consumption.

First, the *true* income of the more disadvantaged is far below their *measured* income—more so than at incomes higher up the scale. If we transplant the median 1957 workers to 1997 and give them a cost-of-living adjustment to make up for inflation between those years, those workers will find some unpleasant changes. Many goods that are called *lumpy* because they cannot be consumed in small units, such as a range of expensive educational and medical services—college tuition and a complete physical exam, for example—are much more expensive now than they were then. In this respect, the choices to be made are harder than in 1957. Thus, homelessness might not have grown so dramatically in recent years were it not that the housing industry is legally required to provide housing in a lump size, not in cubicles.

Goods that have been dubbed *positional*—a home convenient to the office or in a safe neighborhood—tend to rise in price as the incomes of others increase. Thus the workers transplanted from 1957 to 1997 may have to move farther out of town.[3] Finally, there are goods that might be called *social*. We consume them largely, maybe only, because others do. Having a social life requires having a range of common experiences to talk about with others, and that requires being able to afford at least some of the consumer goods the others buy: attendance at sports events, pleasure trips, CDs, videotapes.[4] But more and more of these social goods move out of reach as the income of those higher up the scale increases. As a result of these mechanisms, having a low relative income may impose psychic burdens that impair a worker's ability to use well and enjoy the income he has. (Notice that it is middle-class things that are sought after by the low-paid, not the unimagined, alien lifestyles of the rich.)

Besides, even if the income of the disadvantaged were adequate for subsistence and even for a range of comforts and luxuries, the credit would go not to their wages, which are paltry, but to a cushion of what may be called *social wealth:* the support of relatives and possibly of private charities and, above all, the public entitlements provided to the disadvantaged (along with those for the disabled, the retired, and other nonworking persons). The measure of the cash reward for the *work* supplied by the disadvantaged to the market economy is only their *earnings*. And the *net* reward from this work is only the *excess* of these earnings over the entitlement benefits for which these workers become ineligible as a result of their wage income. Our self-esteem from being self-supporting, not dependent upon the state or kin, hinges on our sense that what we have provided ourselves and our families is largely due to our own efforts. If the net reward is actually negative and large, those low-wage workers with comparably low private wealth may feel themselves too poor to be able to afford the pecuniary sacrifice necessary to "buy" the self-esteem of being self-supporting.

Finally, the disadvantaged worker's prospects for self-realization and social participation—not just income or even earnings—matter enormously, and these prospects may be very poor no matter how reliably the safety net of the welfare system or the family averts material poverty. To have those deeply desired things requires having a productive and visible place in society, hence, for most people, an occupation in the market economy—not work in the underworld or as a domestic concealed from view in someone's home. But the jobs for which disadvantaged workers qualify may be insufficiently rewarding, when measured against the support available if they are not employed, to enlist their energy and dedication. The inducement to work provided by the wage is inherently a *relative* thing. The wage rate is weighed against the options of "welfare," crime, begging, and support by family or spouse. Thus many disadvantaged workers may have only a fragile or sporadic orientation toward jobholding at best. Their performance as employees suffers, which in turn reduces the wages that employers can afford to pay such workers, which causes a further fall of wages and a rise of unemployment as well. With their earnings stream often interrupted by spells of idleness, it becomes even harder for workers facing very low wages to derive fulfillment from their work experience.

The *earnings* of the disadvantaged relative to those of workers further up the scale—say, the working class—can therefore serve as an indicator of the satisfaction these workers can take in their situation. Such a measure of relative earnings is some indication of the likelihood that they will suffer a lack of self-esteem, self-realization, and social participation, a lack of good health, a narrow choice of lumpy goods, a short supply of positional goods, and a deficiency of social consumption. Relative earnings are also some indication of how dependent disadvantaged earners are on other resources—welfare entitlements, support from family and relatives, and the returns from crime and begging.

The Depth of Severe Disadvantage

How large is the class of workers who must go without one or more of the basic middle-class goods? And how extreme does the disadvantage get? To get an idea of the depth of the disadvantage consider the bottom tenth of the labor force. The 1990 census reports that the average hourly wage in the bottom decile—the bottom tenth of those with some earnings in the year—was less than $4. More strikingly, the entire bottom decile earned only $15 billion in 1990, which is about $1,200 per person.[5] (This compares with economy-wide earnings per member of the labor force that year of about $25,000, the gap reflecting the high incidence of unemployment and part-time work among low-wage workers.)

How could 12 million workers have survived on so little? In large part the answer lies in the scale of welfare payments, particularly those for which active and potential workers are eligible—though social security retirement and disability benefits also add to the available pool of social wealth in poor communities. Total public spending for Medicaid, food stamps, housing benefits, and supplemental security income, all of benefit to the employed, came to about $150 billion in the same year. The preponderant part must have gone to those in the bottom tenth. Unemployment insurance benefits and Aid to Families with Dependent Children added $35 billion. Thus the income received under current entitlement programs dwarfs the wage income of those in the bottom decile. We have here a measure of their dependency: they earn only a small fraction of the total income (cash and in-kind income) they receive. But removing the support of the welfare system would not make them independent. At a wage today of $5 an hour, which not all of the bottom tenth can command, they would still be dependent, their dependency shifting to relatives and charities.[6]

A view of the breadth of disadvantage may be obtained by calculating relative earnings at various rungs on the distribution ladder. Consider adult men, aged 25–64, who worked in full-time jobs all or a part of the year. In the late 1980s those at the *top* of the bottom decile—at the tenth percentile—earned little more than 44 percent of what was earned by those at the fiftieth percentile.[7] In today's terms this is a wage a little below $5 an hour. Those at the top of the second decile—the twentieth percentile— earned nearly $6 an hour in today's terms. If we go to the thirtieth percentile, we find an hourly wage around $7—the wage suggested earlier to be at the border of significant disadvantage.

Another Dimension of Disadvantage

In the portrait of disadvantage sketched here there is another dimension that deserves a place: unemployment. The disadvantaged are especially likely to have spells of unemployment. The more advantaged workers take the more stable jobs just as they take the better-paying ones, so disadvantaged workers more often find themselves out of a job. Furthermore, disadvantaged workers, finding the paltry pay less and less of an incentive as their savings accumulate or as some grievance at work mounts up, more often quit or perform at a level that leads eventually to dismissal or relegation to a dead-end job; and these spells "between jobs" tend to be longer for disadvantaged workers.[8]

Data on incidence of unemployment by wage rate are difficult to come by. But there is a strong relationship between wage rate and educational level. (Among male workers in full-time jobs working the full year, those with some college earn 63 percent of what college graduates make, those with just a high school diploma 53 percent, and those with fewer than four years of high school only 40 percent.)[9] And data *are* available on unemployment by level of education.

In 1996 men in the labor force aged 25–64 with a college degree or higher had an unemployment rate of around 2 percent. For those with some college the rate was 4 percent, for those with only a high school degree it was 6 percent, and for those whose education stopped at lower secondary school it was nearly 12 percent.[10]

More striking are the numbers of the working-age disadvantaged who neither are employed in the commercial, above-ground economy nor report themselves as interested in such work. While, among men aged 25–64, only about 5 percent of those with college degrees and 8 percent of those with high school diplomas (or more) are not in the labor force, among men whose education stopped in lower secondary school this number is nearly 25 percent.[11] The participation rates of women are lower at all education levels; nonetheless they also drop off very sharply with decreased education.

We have seen that severe economic deprivation is the rule among the bottom fifth of the labor force and that serious economic disadvantage prevails among most of the bottom third. The data exaggerate the phenomenon in one respect, since low wages are only temporary for some; but the data also understate the phenomenon, since they do not take account of the emotional burdens of working for paltry reward. The low employment rates of the least advantaged are, to some extent, evidence that many able-bodied and competent persons have been demoralized, at least for a time, by the poverty of their opportunities.

These facts are awkward for proponents of free-market doctrine. In that philosophy, economic policy need do nothing to enable and encourage work and self-support, since all those who are able and competent, if they act responsibly, will do well enough in the marketplace. (For the weak and the sick a generous welfare program of disability benefits and social security insurance is in order.) For decades, free-market proponents could argue with some plausibility that, even if pockets of disadvantage remained in our country, the depth of poverty experienced in them was lessening and the pockets were rapidly shrinking, thanks to economic growth and the increased education that accompanied it. Developments over the past generation, however, have raised serious questions about the reliability and timeliness of that process.

3

■

The Decline of Labor

It is a fallacy that normal economic processes operate to pull up wage rates at the low end relative to those in the middle—that is, to erode inequality. When Francis Galton observed the heights of fathers and sons, he saw that the sons of short men tended to be less short (and the sons of tall men less tall). But this does not mean that, over generations, heights tend to equalize; natural shocks are continually replenishing the genetic pool with extreme cases. Similarly, the well-documented upward mobility of poor families from generation to generation does not imply any tendency for wages of the unskilled to catch up to the median wage. The economic shocks sending some people to the bottom of the heap may be just strong enough to offset the upward climb of low earners, so that the distribution of wages is unchanged. Or, the balance between these opposing forces may shift for or against the relative position of low earners until stability is regained for a while.

Henry George, in contrast, based his American classic *Progress and Poverty* on his argument that economic growth propelled the privileged ever farther above the unprivileged. (He thought landowners monopolized the gains from technological advances.) Economists are pretty sure that the share of the pie earned by the bottom groups has not followed a downward trend. It has been struck by permanent shocks, though.

In the 1940s the position of low earners relative to median wage earners improved strikingly. This was the decade of the Great Wage Compression. (A recent investigation traces nearly half of this phenomenon to developments in the public sector.) But then in the 1950s relative wages of low-wage men began a long downhill slide. Among women, a similar slide started in the late 1980s. The median wage has also lost ground over the past generation to higher-paid labor—and to capital. The past quarter-century has brought an end to an era of good wages at the low end.[1]

The Broad Decline of Relative Wages

During the 1950s, when low-wage workers were thought to be gaining ground, the average wage of *men* in *full-time* jobs in the bottom pay echelons fell about 2½ percent relative to the median wage. Then they fell another 4 percent behind the pack in the 1960s. This widening of the gap between the bottom and the middle reflected the decline of strongback labor. Low-wage men fell behind by another 9 percent in the 1970s and by nearly 10 percent in the 1980s.[2] They lost ground at about the same rate in the early 1990s, then stabilized in 1995. As a result, the relative wage was back at its 1940 level by the mid-1970s and was nearly 20 percent below that level by the mid-1990s.

Up to the mid-1970s these relative declines were not large enough to add up to an absolute decline of wages. In the 1960s, for example, the median wage rose by 23 percent. The relative decline of 4 percent therefore amounted to an absolute *increase* of 19 percent. But in the 1970s the median wage grew at only 7 percent, so the relative decline of 9 percent meant an absolute *decrease* of 2 percent. In the 1980s even the *median* wage fell—by 7 percent. Hence the 10 percent relative decline meant a huge absolute decline of 17 percent. There is no reason to expect the relative decline to be made up. The odds that it will get a good deal worse are not much longer than the odds that it will appreciably recover.

For another perspective on the earning power of disadvantaged workers we may consider the relative wages of the less educated. Among white men in either full-time or part-time jobs, the average annual earnings of high school graduates fell by 3.3 percent between the mid-1960s and the mid-1980s, while those of high school dropouts declined far more, by 17.1 percent. As a result, the percentage gap, which was already appreciable, approximately doubled.

The same falling away of earnings in the bottom half of the distribution can be viewed more directly—in terms of the relative earnings levels at selected points in the earnings distribution. Consider the distribution of earnings of *all* adult male workers, full-time, part-time, and self-employed. Those workers at the tenth percentile in 1986 earned only 35 percent of what the median workers earned. But this represented a sharp decline from 1979, when the tenth percentile earned 41 percent of median earnings. The decline of those at the twentieth percentile was nearly as large, from 59 percent in 1979 to 54 percent in 1986.[3] These relative declines continued up to the mid-1990s, judging by preliminary data, so the cumulative declines up to the mid-1990s are substantially larger.

Wages have also declined in the middle of the distribution—approximately at the border between the working class and the middle class—relative to those farther up the scale. This decline resembles the experience of the lowest-paid. The wages of men in the middle quintile gained 10 percent on those in the next-to-highest decile in the 1940s, held this gain over the next decade, gave up half of it in the 1960s, fell back by another 2 percent in the 1970s and by another 4 percent in the 1980s.

All the declines among the disadvantaged are broad-based, extending to old and young and to whites, Hispanics, and blacks. But not to women. The absolute deterioration in the wages of disadvantaged women did not begin until the late 1980s. Their wages were narrowing the gap with the median wages of men throughout this postwar period. Female high school graduates did see a decline in wages relative to those of female college graduates, but it was much smaller than the corresponding relative decline among men.[4]

The Broad Decline of Employment

Levels of employment have also declined over the past generation. The declines have consisted of both a decrease in labor force participation (which includes both employed and unemployed workers) and an increase in unemployment within the labor force.

Unemployment has increased considerably among several categories within the labor force, women as well as men. The unemployment rate of adults (aged 25—64) in the bottom educational category—those without a high school degree—rose from about $4\frac{1}{2}$ percent in 1970 to around 11 percent in 1987 and $12\frac{1}{2}$ percent in 1994. The rate for adult men in that bottom category rose still more, from 4 percent in 1970 to around 11 percent in 1987 to almost 13 percent by 1994. (Thus the men's rate caught up with that for women.) The unemployment rate of adult male high school graduates also rose, from about $2\frac{1}{2}$ percent in 1970 to around $5\frac{1}{2}$ percent in 1989 and around 7 percent in 1994. College graduates did not escape either. Their unemployment rate—for men and women together—went from around 2 percent in the early 1970s to not quite 3 percent in the mid-1990s.[5] Although a substantial proportionate increase, it is quite small relative to their labor force participation (which is what matters).

Readers who are familiar with the history of the *general* unemployment rate over the same period may detect a paradox in these figures. The increase in the average unemployment rate was much smaller over the same period—from around 5 percent in the early 1970s to somewhat less than 6 percent in 1995. The rate among adult men went from 3 percent to 5 percent.[6] How to explain the disparity between these modest increases and the extraordinary ones in each educational category? The answer at a purely arithmetical level is that over the past generation more and more of the labor force have migrated to higher educational categories—taking weight from a category of higher unemployment and giving it to a category of lower unemployment.

But it would be wrong to conclude from that alone that the rise of education is a force acting to reduce the general unemployment rate. It *could* be that the attainment of higher levels of education by an increased number within the labor force placed them in jobs where they were less susceptible to unemployment, while in each educational category there was no improvement at all—and no worsening either. That would be an immensely important finding. It would mean that many of the less disadvantaged are making costly investments to reclaim some lost ground.

But there are other possibilities. One of them reminds me of the Harvard economist Thomas Schelling's image of the student who, in leaving Harvard for Yale, "raised the average in both places." It may be that those who make it up the educational ladder pull up the unemployment rate of the category they leave, where they were relatively good at avoiding unemployment, and yet raise the unemployment rate of the category they join, since they are relatively prone to unemployment in that more rarified company. For their additional education to contribute to reducing the general unemployment rate it is necessary that, with increased education, they become less prone to unemployment than they were before. It is also necessary that their added education does not aggravate too much the frequency of unemployment among those who do not get more education. No one can be sure that these conditions are satisfied. A preliminary analysis by Gylfi Zoega and me does suggest, though, that increased educational attainment of the American labor force has in fact helped a lot to reduce the general unemployment rate.[7]

The decline of participation in the labor force is the other part of the fall in employment over the past generation. Appreciable numbers of the disadvantaged have given up trying to land a job in the market sector. From the point of view of the rest of society, nonparticipation in the labor force is worse in a way than unemployment, since when some workers of a certain type drop out of the labor force, the number employed will decrease (in proportion to the number unemployed) as the economy regains the equilibrium *rate* of unemployment for such workers. (Approximately, the departing unemployed must be replaced out of the ranks of the employed.) In reaction it might be contended that this does not matter for the rest of society, since when the disadvantaged elect to leave the labor force it is their own income that suffers. But the rest of society is left with a larger share of the tax burden and an increased welfare burden.

In the case of young disadvantaged men, nonparticipation poses special social costs. A significant number of the disadvantaged men have left poorly paying jobs or left the unemployment pool for illegal activities. There are no data on the number of full-time and part-time criminals. We do know, however, that there has been a strong rise in criminal convictions and in the rate of incarceration. A million and a half persons, mostly men, are now in prison—one in fifty men of working age.[8] Many others are awaiting trial, either in jail or out on bail, or are on parole from prison. It is said that in several American cities nearly half the young black men are under the administration of the criminal justice system.

Of course, not all the nonmarket and nondomestic activity of able-bodied working-age persons is illegal. There is also an informal economy of street vending, bartering, and brokering—hustling, in other words. Much of this activity, also called the underground economy, survives through the nonpayment of taxes and rent not easily escaped by participants in what is usually called the market sector—more aptly, the legitimate enterprise sector.

The declines in men's labor force participation are far steeper than is generally realized. Among men with less than a high school education the participation rate went from 87 percent in 1973 to about 77 percent in 1989. The participation rate of men in the same age group who completed high school but did not attend college also slipped, from 95 percent in 1973 to 90 percent in 1989.[9]

In the economy-wide measures of economic activity—the *gen-*

eral unemployment rate and the *overall* labor force participation rate—we see far smaller changes. As already noted, the general unemployment rate went up only a percentage point or a little more over the past three decades. It may be, as mentioned earlier, that the increased education of the labor force has served to brake the rise of unemployment. Another factor, however, is that women as a group do not show an increased tendency toward unemployment over the past generation. The rate for adult women actually dropped between 1980 and 1995—from 6 percent to around 4 percent. Women were not immune to the general weakening of the market for labor: the unemployment rate of women with less than a high school education rose from a little more than 5½ percent in 1970 to around 12½ percent in 1994, a rise that approaches the one for men in the same educational category. Among women with college degrees there was also a trace of an increase in unemployment over these two decades. However, the fraction of women in the labor force with college degrees increased, so women's overall unemployment rate could drop while the rates in each category rose.

The overall participation rate among adults aged 25–64 did not decline—it actually rose from around 60 percent to around 66 percent. The opposing trend in women's participation in the labor force holds the main explanation, beyond any doubt. Women's participation rate continued to climb in spite of the weakening of the labor market, rising from 50 percent in 1973 to 70 percent in 1993, where it stabilized.

Declines in Labor's Share of Productive Rewards

Looking at the economy as a whole, we see a decline stretching over two decades in hourly labor cost relative to hourly productivity—that is, relative to total output per hour worked. In other words, the part of the economy's output that employers pay to labor—in the form of take-home wages, noncash supplements, and payroll taxes paid by employer and employee—has declined as a share of total output. In the two good years 1972 and 1973, this share averaged 66.6 percent in the corporate sector. In the next pair of back-to-back good years, 1988 and 1989, it averaged 65.5 percent. In the latest such pair of years, 1994 and 1995, it was around 64 percent. Such a shrinkage may seem small. But the share of output earned by labor rather than land or capital has long been regarded as one of the great constants of the American economy and economies everywhere.[10] So the further shrinkage in recent years is notable enough to be front-page news.[11]

This slow erosion of labor's share can be compared with global warming. Just as the gradual rise in the earth's temperature is of little consequence for most people but serious for the Bangladesh villages it puts under water, so the decline of labor's share matters little for most members of the labor force but may critically undermine the labor force participation or the job attachment of those whose wages were already marginal.

Labor's share has not sunk quite as low as it was from the early 1950s until the mid-1960s. However, it will sink below the 1950s level if the trend of the past two decades continues a few years more.[12]

So much for labor's gross share. There has been a much stronger relative decline in labor's compensation net of payroll tax—in take-home pay and noncash supplements, or fringe benefits. Payroll taxes drive a wedge between what is received by the employee (wages and supplements net of payroll tax) and what is paid by the employer (wages and supplements plus payroll tax). As many remember it, these taxes ballooned during Lyndon Johnson's presidency to finance the Great Society. According to other recollections, the increase came with Richard Nixon's generosity to the elderly. In fact, payroll taxes climbed steadily from the late 1960s to the early 1980s and have continued to rise at a slower pace since then. The wedge between compensation paid and compensation received has expanded from 8 percent (of compensation paid) in 1965 to 10 percent in 1970 to 12½ percent in the mid-1970s and on to 15½ percent in the 1990s.

An expanding wedge may come partly at the expense of capital in the short run, pushing up labor's gross share (leaving a shrunken share for capital) while weighing down labor's net share to some extent too. But in the long run capital has to get a return that corresponds to the cost of capital given by world interest rates—or no investment will be forthcoming. A range of evidence points to the conclusion that capital's share is resistant to the wedge in the long run, leaving labor's net share to bear the whole of the adjustment. And in fact labor's net share has experienced a steep, fifteen-year fall, from as high as 60 percent in the early 1970s to around 53 percent in 1995.

This payroll tax wedge is not a total loss in the reward to jobholding. Some portion of the revenue raised by payroll taxes makes possible an addition to the nonwage benefit available to those persons with long careers in the labor force. On the surface, the revenues from payroll taxes are all earmarked for administration of the unemployment insurance funds and for the Social Security Administration, which, operating on a pay-as-you-go basis, uses these proceeds to finance its outlays for retirement benefits and disability benefits—and for no other purpose. But had no such unemployment, retirement, and disability benefit system been instituted, the previous nonsystem of emergency relief and charity would have continued to develop, financed out of other tax revenues or philanthropic funds. Hence the amount of social support that the system of unemployment, retirement, and disability benefits has added is only a fraction of what it spends; the remaining fraction simply lightens the burden on other government and philanthropic resources, which can then finance other sorts of expenditures—expenditures that, as valuable as they may be, add nothing to the rewards from employment. (We have the protection of the Pentagon and the Attorney General whether we work or not.)

A further slippage between tax paid and benefit received arises from the poor design of the system. Employees still far away from retirement today see their employee tax (and their employer's matching tax) as an investment offering a poorer return than they could obtain if they could invest it themselves. The prospective rate of return on this investment, after all, is about equal to the economy's rate of growth, no more than 2½ percent per year. In contrast, several types of mutual funds seem likely to deliver a rate of return, adjusted for inflation, between 3 and 4 percent per annum. And low-wage workers must figure on a higher mortality rate than that of the general population.

In just two generations we have seen a major setback in the reward to work of disadvantaged men relative to the median wage. The deterioration began slowly in the 1950s, gathered speed in the 1960s, and has cumulated in a decline in the relative wage of nearly one-third since 1950. This decline has had demoralizing effects that must in many cases have amplified its burdensomeness on disadvantaged workers: unemployment among the less educated has skyrocketed, despite the partial recovery of the general unemployment rate, as reduced job attachment among many low-paid men has spelled increased turnover. Labor force participation by less educated men has fallen markedly, as they have been moved to try the informal or underground sector. Increasing numbers of the least advantaged have landed in prison, as many engaged in crime have been caught and convicted.

This record matters—it is not enough to know where we have got, regardless of how we got there. It is part of our folklore that, in America, whatever may happen elsewhere, the less fortunate regularly narrow the gap between themselves and those in society's mainstream. But that myth seems, in fact, to have American history upside down: it was in the nineteenth century that inclusion, self-support, and social cohesion were in full flower, if standard sources such as Tocqueville can be relied on; in these respects, the twentieth century, for all its progress in civil rights and tolerance, is problematic. If this is so, ever-higher stages of economic accomplishment do not guarantee improvement in the social position of relatively low-wage labor. Time, or progress, is not to be counted on the side of the less advantaged.

Some theorists optimistically view economic growth as nonetheless helpful to the disadvantaged: if we run faster we won't remain in the same place but will reach a better place. But here too the record is not encouraging. With strain we can imagine a return to the rapid growth rate (about 2½ percent annually) of the early postwar decades. As noted in this chapter, however, the gradual separation of the rewards to disadvantaged labor from those in the middle was occurring even in the 1950s and 1960s. In short, it may be that the disadvantaged would do better in relation to others if the economy began to grow faster. But the historical record does not suggest that this effect could ever be strong enough to rescue those workers and discouraged workers now operating at the margins of society.

4

∎

The Damage to Others

When serious economic disadvantage strikes workers, the worst casualties are likely to be the workers themselves. But the impact may send strong shock waves reaching others—their families, their neighborhoods, and the society as a whole.

Damage to Children

The offspring of disadvantaged workers are often among the most adversely affected. A family is a kind of school for living, but one that is only as good as its teachers. When parents are poor earners, possibly jobless at times, and hence frequently or always dependent on welfare, one of the more serious consequences is that they are not in a position to be good role models for their children. Children are unlikely to be able to acquire from such parents the habits of initiative and responsibility they will need to succeed in the labor force. When we read about someone who *has* overcome serious disadvantages, particularly family disadvantages, he or she usually turns out to have had a mentor, often a teacher, who filled the place that is normally taken by parents. This is the familiar "cycle of poverty."

Economic disadvantage plays a part, together with the welfare system, in creating families without fathers. A woman who does not find a potential husband able to support a family may decide against marriage and yet have children, a decision made possible by the state support to which she will be entitled. The children thus grow up without the support of a two-parent family. Hard choices among alternative privations then have to be made. If the mother decides to remain at home with the children she will consign them to subsisting on what is provided by welfare and deny herself the satisfactions of employment. If she decides to hold a job or two, her income net of the costs of childcare and reduced eligibility for welfare may show little gain or even a loss, and she will have less time to give attention and affection to her children. Either way, the children of one-parent families may reach their adult years more disadvantaged for a life as productive and responsible citizens than their counterparts were in the previous generation. A force is operating, then, to make economic disadvantage actually worsen from one generation to the next.

Those who look on the bright side can point to a mechanism that may slow the decline of the disadvantaged and ultimately stabilize their situation. As their relative wages fall, many may find that the gap between their wage and the wage they expect they could obtain by getting more education has widened in absolute (not just percentage) terms. These disadvantaged workers will have a stronger and stronger incentive to increase their investment in education—to finish high school or to attend college—in the hope of clambering off the down escalator onto one going up (or at any rate one not going down as rapidly).[1]

But this mechanism seems to have faltered in recent years. During the 1970s the percentage of workers aged 25–29 who had completed high school continued its historic climb, reaching 85 percent (from 78 percent). No further gain has occurred since that decade, despite the decline in the wages of high school dropouts relative to those of graduates. A similar halt occurred in the percentage of the same cohort of workers having a college diploma.[2] It may be that the stimulus to finish high school provided by the *relative* decline in wages of the dropouts has been outweighed by a decline in the *absolute* decline they observe in the wages of those who do complete high school; after all, it is the absolute *difference* between the diploma holder's wage and the dropout's wage that a teenager is going to consider and to compare with the various costs of pursuing the diploma. (Another factor is the rate of interest, which has been generally quite elevated from the early 1980s onward.)

In any case some say that this mechanism is not without a social cost. The French economist Gilles Saint-Paul suggests that the acquisition of vocational skills by some makes things worse for those left behind. When typists learn word-processing skills, each of them is transformed into two or three or more typists of the standard type. The supply of labor in standardized units is effectively augmented, as if more unskilled competitors had been injected into the labor market. If what is called diminishing returns sets in (as increased labor power does not find increased land and capital to work with), the piece rate employers can afford to pay per thousand words processed is driven down. Those whose capability has not increased therefore find their hourly wage driven down in equal proportion.

Fortunately, Saint-Paul's view is much less applicable to countries open to global trade and capital movements. Our economy is wide open, so increases of capital can rush in from abroad to work with increased labor. But it is not certain that the global economy has grown so large that it tends to erase completely what happens here.[3]

Damage to the Neighborhood

As disadvantaged workers have become more urban, along with the rest of the population, they have concentrated in large urban neighborhoods. Racial segregation is usually invoked to explain the concentrations of poor blacks, and undoubtedly anti-black biases in the housing market tend to reinforce segregation. However, we also observe similar concentrations of ethnic groups, many of which are not subject to biases excluding them from other neighborhoods. Presumably these racial and ethnic concentrations serve as a kind of support group. (Ethologists such as

W. D. Hamilton find self-interest in concentration of population, but that does not mean it is collectively best or costless.)

Unfortunately the massing of disadvantaged persons into large, high-density groups exposes them to some further adversities. Relatively low wages and relatively high rates of joblessness, concentrated in an urban area, may have devastating effects on the whole neighborhood.

A discriminatory mechanism operates to transmit the poor opportunities of the disadvantaged to others in their community—a discrimination based on lack of information, not racial or ethnic antagonism or any deep-seated prejudice. When there are a large number of workers in a neighborhood whose tenuous job attachments, growing out of their personal circumstances or their vulnerability to social conditions, have made them unreliable employees, they give the neighborhood a bad reputation as a source of reliable employees—the more so the larger their proportion.

If most or all employers had all the information they could want about each job applicant, neighborhood reputation would not count—a good applicant's true promise would shine through. But employers must hire workers without complete information, and accordingly they will hold it against an applicant that he or she comes from a bad neighborhood.[4] The sociologist William Julius Wilson has shown that having an address in the Robert Taylor Holmes project in Chicago stigmatizes job applicants as likely to be unreliable.[5] The labor market has to be very tight to induce an employer to accept such poor bets.

Information plays the central role in another mechanism operating to spread and magnify economic disadvantage. Where the preponderance of workers are seriously disadvantaged, most of them lacking access to high-wage business enterprises, there are few channels through which younger workers may gain information about newly opened jobs.

One might expect that entrepreneurs, eyeing the cheap labor in the inner city, would find it in their interest to open businesses in poor neighborhoods, thus removing the obstacles that entrants to the labor force living there previously faced in learning of opportunities. In fact poor communities lack start-up enterprises with anything like the density found in other communities. Much blame is laid on the banks, which are accused of redlining black neighborhoods. (It is said, however, that the default rate on loans to black-owned businesses actually exceeds that on loans to white-owned firms, which suggests that the banks have erred on the side of reverse discrimination to avoid suspicion of redlining.) Another speculation is that the historical background of slavery from which black Americans emerged little more than a century ago still militates against the rise of entrepreneurship. The true explanation may be that the dearth of entrepreneurship is more an effect than a cause of underdevelopment. (Some observers add, though, that an anti-business attitude existing in inner cities and fed by some community leaders has scared entrepreneurs away.)

In a community where success is a rarity, young people are likely to have low expectations of what can be gained by more initiative or hard work. (There are also uncertainties clouding the returns.) Young people who know, say, just one success story may suspect that it is too unrepresentative to be applicable to themselves. And they may fear that beyond the first hurdle there are many more hurdles of unknown difficulty, so there is little point in starting. Thus an atmosphere of rational defeatism tends to develop. Teenagers and young adults are the most vulnerable here, of course. The only effect operating in reverse is that those who feel they might be able to do much better than the average may be made more determined to get out. Unfortunately, this self-preserving exodus from the neighborhood makes things worse for those who stay behind.

The welfare state operates in the same way. When a rich society puts up a comfortable safety net it reduces the distance between the outcome that the seriously disadvantaged can expect from making an extra effort and what the safety net will provide them if they do not make the effort. The sense of futility undermines people's willingness to try to improve their circumstances. This general tendency reduces the normal level of initiative, risk-taking, and hard work in the community.

In principle each young person should make his or her own

thoughtful decision about whether to make a run for economic success. But not everyone who would otherwise try will have the emotional strength to deviate from the neighborhood norm. Doing so may be taken by one's circle of friends as a betrayal, a violation of the implicit pact to fail together. Thus the psychology of failure is reinforced by social ties.

With most in the neighborhood feeling alienated from the economic mainstream, feeling powerless to do better, and feeling that even normal effort brings little gain, it is no puzzle that drug use is relatively widespread in these communities. Drug addiction in turn induces the user to turn into a supplier recruiting new addicts in order to support his addiction.

The atmosphere of failure, the significant drug use, and substantial drug trade combine to generate a high level of criminality in disadvantaged neighborhoods. Incidents of theft and violence are common. Criminals have guns and a great many others acquire them out of fear. As the bleak prospect of the disadvantaged reduces what they are willing to pay for their own lives, it also reduces the value they place on others' lives. It is not surprising that some of the disadvantaged, feeling they are not respected by society, seek "respect" through the use of guns. This grim and violent environment makes it difficult for children to stay clear of drugs, guns, and crime. As standards erode, children become involved with these things at ever earlier ages. (The number of murders committed by youths aged 14–17 increased by 165 percent in the ten years ending in 1994.)[6]

All this is being acted out daily in urban high schools in which the pupils come largely from disadvantaged neighborhoods. These schools are thus obstructed in their mission to provide students with the education they will need if they are later to secure good jobs in the business world.

Damage to the Society

The relatively low wages and relatively frequent joblessness of the disadvantaged also have several adverse impacts extending beyond the neighborhood and community to the society as a whole.

As a result the rest of society pays a high cost for the incidence of serious economic disadvantage in its midst.

Through the ordinary operation of markets, the pathologies suffered by the disadvantaged—their depressed employment and underinvestment in their capabilities—also harm the advantaged participants in the economy. This proposition has its roots in a standard and uncontroversial relationship sometimes clouded by misunderstandings. The aggregate income of high-skilled labor and land is significantly increased by the collaboration of low-skilled labor in the economy's production, just as the aggregate income of the labor in a one-skill or two-skill economy is boosted by an abundance of land to work with.[7] (In essence, the low-skilled bring a mix of resources to the economy's activity different from that of the high-skilled, and the resulting exchanges are beneficial for both groups.) The Oscar winners who in their speeches thank tens of others are a great deal more realistic than the radical individualists who imagine that their success owes nothing to the rest of society.

Unfortunately the contribution of the disadvantaged to the advantaged is diluted at present by their high unemployment and their depressed participation in the labor force. Their contribution may be further drained by their very low productivity—the dearth of skills and dedication they bring to employers. (The relatively low wage rate of a great many workers in this country is, after all, an indication of their low productivity—the ineffectiveness of their labor input in generating revenue for businesses.) And in the past generation their productivity has fallen even lower, if their sinking hourly wage is an indication.[8]

As a result, their input into the economy generates less for others—just as it generates less for themselves. If the bottom third of workers today earn only one-tenth of the total wages in the economy, it is a reasonable guess that their labor added one-fifth *of that* to the wages of other workers and the rent on land—hence one-fiftieth of total wages. Whatever the correct amount, it would be a much larger figure if the country undertook an economic policy to engage the disadvantaged fully in the market economy. (Chapter 9 totes up costs and benefits in this regard and others.)

The low earnings of the disadvantaged also entail a loss of tax revenue, a cost to other taxpayers who then have to shoulder a larger share of the fiscal burden. Two other burdens of economic disadvantage borne by the rest of society are the costs of law enforcement and of the welfare state. Clearly the citizens outside disadvantaged neighborhoods are not unaffected by the social pathologies—the high drug use and high crime rates. Distance provides some protection, but a small distance only small protection. The mass exodus of the well-off in recent decades from the big metropolitan areas of the Northeast and Midwest to the low-density areas of the Southwest can be interpreted as an effort to put greater distance between themselves and concentrations of low-wage workers.

A significant part of the defense against crime and the drug trade is undertaken by the government. Its cost is also huge: police protection and correction costs have been running at about 6 percent of total government purchases of goods and services, 20 percent of nondefense government purchases, and a little more than one percent of national income (or the net national product) in recent years. Expenditures for the administration of the criminal justice system are nearly as large, having nearly doubled in the 1980s.[9] Much of this expense could be saved if the extremely low earnings and depressed employment of the disadvantaged were remedied.

Connecting these huge expenses to serious economic disadvantage is a matter of interpretation, of course. From time immemorial, however, the existence of *some* relationship has been common wisdom. ("Where Enterprise thrives / Crime can never begin," as Tamino says in *The Magic Flute*.) But present-day observers point out that there is no sure-fire and universal relation between straitened circumstances and social pathology. Most people down on their luck do not commit crimes.[10] The 1930s was the classic period of abysmally low wages and severely depressed employment, and yet it did not produce the social breakdown that had become so visible by the 1970s. The streets of New York were safe, Harlem included.[11] Evidently adverse economic forces are not sufficient to bring down communities.

A clue to the puzzle may be that the declines of employment and of wages in the 1930s were nationwide. Investors on Wall Street jumped to their death from office windows in the years following the stock market crash of 1929. Congress passed a series of bills aimed at providing a "New Deal" for the jobless and the low-paid. So the feeling of exclusion from society that, it seems reasonable to assume, would otherwise have spread among the disadvantaged was largely averted. (Yet the government in those times was more willing to use force: MacArthur's troops fired on demonstrating squatters in the nation's capital, and the streets were more closely policed.)

Another clue to the puzzle is that the Great Depression was over within a decade. Now, in contrast, deprivation and idleness have been fixtures of poor communities for decades and have only worsened in the past generation. This long period has provided these economic conditions with ample time to weaken institutions of socialization, such as family and school, that had been bulwarks against crime and drugs.

Whatever the channels of causation, the statistical associations between economic disadvantage and indicators of crime and drug addiction are persuasive enough. In the cities where the robbery rate per inhabitant is highest (Miami, Newark, Atlanta, New York, Detroit, Tampa, Washington, Chicago, Jersey City, and St. Louis) the fraction of the labor force with low wages is large, and where the robbery rate is lowest (Mesa, Virginia Beach, Honolulu, Anchorage, Colorado Springs, San Jose, Lexington, Aurora, Omaha, and Austin) that fraction appears to be much smaller.[12] There are classic works showing the correlation between the ups and downs of the unemployment rate and various crime rates.[13] Property crime is observed to go up with the protractedness of unemployment.

The last cost of economic disadvantage borne by the rest of society is the outlays to the disadvantaged under the entitlement programs of the welfare state. Beginning with Bismarck in Germany and Roosevelt in this country, it has been a mainstay of social policy that job losers are entitled to unemployment benefits.

Later the idea of compensation for misfortune was extended to the disabled and—upon application of a means test—the sick, the homeless, and those with dependent children.

The rationale was inspired by the insurance principle that shipowners have long used to share among them the loss from shipwrecks caused by natural disasters and acts of God. However, social policy determined that unemployment insurance, unlike ship insurance, would be neither private nor voluntary; the fear was that, if workers were given discretion to buy or not to buy insurance on the private market, a disproportionate share of those who knew they were prone to unemployment would insure themselves, thus unfairly driving up the cost to others and discouraging them from buying the insurance—a problem known as adverse selection. The same logic was applied to all the other entitlement programs.

However, public funding does not avoid the problem of adverse selection; the taxpayers are assessed all of the costs even though the majority pay more in taxes for the program than their expectation of benefits could possibly be worth to them. Furthermore, with the suppliers of insurance no longer compelled to reject applicants with a poor track record, there was little in the way of checks against abuses of the system: workers assured of state unemployment benefits might move more heavily into cyclically unstable work, and persons expecting state aid if their house burned down might build in areas known to be fire risks. Thus the insurance problem of moral hazard was added to the problem of adverse selection.

The social insurance programs mainly benefitting the disadvantaged are, leaving unemployment compensation and a few other programs aside, primarily those subject to a means test. It has been calculated that about 2½ percent of the gross domestic product—or about 3 percent of national income—is spent by the government under means-tested programs of social insurance.[14] These are not large sums relative to what the advantaged part of society can afford to pay. They are colossal sums, however, relative to the earnings of the disadvantaged. Hence they have tremendous power to do good or harm by affecting the structure of incentives facing disadvantaged persons of working age.

But whether, as is argued forcefully by some, the welfare system has done more harm than good is not the crucial question. (It may be readily agreed that the welfare system in general, and the unemployment compensation program in particular, have had costly side effects: in providing entitlements to a range of the idle, including the unemployed, the government weakens their incentives to take a job or to hang onto the job they have.) That question is whether the gargantuan sums spent on welfare, crime prevention, drug control, and imprisonment are the best use for that money.

The major difficulty with a social policy limited to programs founded on the insurance principle is that, even where their benefits are tied to acceptance of retraining, these programs do little or nothing to remedy the depressed employment and pay that prevent workers from being self-supporting. The entitlement philosophy does not and cannot go beyond the ancient shipowners' idea of insurance in responding to apparently unpreventable acts of God—one worker's dislocation, another's obsolescence. But mass idleness and deprivation, and the social pathologies they breed, are not like that. By taking constructive actions governments can move unemployment rates down and pull up the lower wage rates by large amounts—just as ill-considered policies have in some countries caused increases in joblessness and relative declines in wages on a large scale.

The Causes

■

5

.

Is It Culture?

Many observers see high joblessness and low wages in our society as partly the result of cultural forces. Some say that the sharp decline of work and of relative wages among the low-paid in recent decades is the effect of a decline of morals. Some say that large parts of the low-wage population have been disadvantaged by a distinctive culture. Some view cultural biases against racial and ethnic groups as a factor holding back numerous low-wage workers. These cultural forces are routinely assumed to limit the effectiveness of economic policy (taxes and subsidies) as a way to draw in and pull up disadvantaged groups. In the extreme view, only cultural policy (motivational courses, religious programs, sensitivity training, and so forth) goes to the heart of the matter.

In the discussion of the depth and breadth of economic disadvantage in this country and its worsening over recent decades, economists and most social scientists have paid little attention to culture. We need to take a critical look at the contentions coming from the cultural perspective.

In popular discussion it is often taken for granted that many of the poor owe much of their poverty to their attitudes toward work and that a deterioration of these attitudes lies behind some of the decline in employment and perhaps even some of the fall of their wages over the past generation. Economists can agree that poor

51

attitudes toward work, where they occur, have detrimental effects whether or not culture is really the cause of the change in attitudes.

Education is one channel through which attitudes can penalize. People who in their formative years do not believe that their work opportunities will be of much value to them are likely to invest less time and money in their education on this account. Thus they will be less able in their adult years to pick up the skills needed to earn good wages. The low pay and the poor prospects for future pay raises are likely in turn to affect their morale, with the result that their participation in the labor force is not sustained and their capacity to perform well in entry-level jobs is impaired.

There is another channel running from work attitudes to earnings. Where the diligence and perseverance of workers are low, employment is bound to fall and unemployment to rise. Even in the supply-and-demand story of neoclassical economics, frequent shuttling out of and back into the labor force obviously cuts into employment and earnings. The modern theory of wages and unemployment brings in the hazards to the employer of poor job attachment and performance by employees and the effects of employers' resort to "incentive wages" as a remedy. This theory argues that when some workers become more prone to quit or shirk their duties, higher production costs result. Either productivity, as measured by output per employee, is *down* or, as employers attempt to outpay one another in hopes of improving their employees' commitment to the job, the going wage level is *up*—or both. (The increased costs cannot be offset by a pay cut since that would reduce productivity by worsening employee performance as much as it reduced hourly wages.) The cost increase prompts employers to suspend hiring until unemployment has increased enough to shrink costs back to the sustainable level—until productivity and wage are back in balance.[1] But then some workers will be unable to gain employment at the market wage.

Unreliable job attachment and performance of employees may also decrease wages—while decreasing employment at the same time.[2] If the propensity of a class of workers to quit, shirk, and so on increases, their productivity is thereby reduced; and though the worsened employee performance will prompt some boost in the incentive wage, that initial increase may aim far short of fully restoring productivity. In that case, as unemployment rises in response to the cost pressure, causing the incentive wage to decline and (possibly) productivity to rise, the level at which wage and productivity reunite may be lower than their level before.[3] So it may well be that poor attitudes toward work help explain the low wages of the disadvantaged and the sag in their relative wages over the past generation.

Cultural Sources of Poor Attitudes toward Work

But is the much deplored deterioration in attitudes toward work of cultural origin? One might look for sources of poorer attitudes in a variety of noncultural developments.

A commonplace noncultural hypothesis is that the steep upward trend in the standard of living in all social strata over the century from the 1870s until the mid-1970s imparted an upward trend in unemployment and downward trend in labor force participation—along with a shorter workweek and a drift toward more pleasant work. The evidence goes against this hypothesis, though. The near-century of annual unemployment rates in the United Kingdom from 1861 to 1957 reported in a famous study by the New Zealand economist-engineer William Phillips showed no systematic rise at all. In the United States, the unemployment rate was not much higher in the mid-1960s, when inflation was steady, than in the early 1890s, when inflation was likewise steady. Poorer attitudes toward work do not appear to be an inevitable byproduct of economic development.[4]

A different noncultural hypothesis fares much better. It states that attitudes toward work have been worsened by the fall in workers' *wages* relative to their overall *wealth*. This wealth includes their private wealth, of course, and also what I have been calling their social wealth: their access to parents or others willing and able to provide support and their entitlements under various government programs. (The disadvantaged—say, the bottom third of the labor force—are not rolling in private wealth. Yet they have become better cushioned against a long spell of unemployment than their predecessors in the 1950s or the 1920s, which helps to explain why unemployment could reach such low levels in those times. About one-third of American families in the bottom quintile of the income distribution now own their own homes.)

The wage-wealth ratio took a double hit: one factor was wages, which rose much more slowly and less equally in the late 1970s and 1980s, eventually halting or even declining. The other factor was the expansion of the welfare state—everything from social assistance (such as food stamps and Medicaid) to social security (for the aged and disabled)—in the 1960s and 1970s. When the reward from work goes down and the need to work goes down too, and they do so most strongly among a group of workers whose reward from working is already precariously low, it is not surprising that many of them manifest negative attitudes toward their jobs and toward jobholding in general. No wonder, then, that it was in the span between the early 1970s and the mid-1980s that unemployment made its sustained climb to a higher plateau and national net private saving went from $9\frac{1}{4}$ percent of national income (in 1970) to $5\frac{3}{4}$ percent (in 1990).[5]

However, this is an economic and political explanation of worsened attitudes toward work among the disadvantaged, not a cultural explanation. A culturalist interpretation of the apparent disaffection with work (and of the resulting decline of employment and wages) has to attribute it to cultural factors, not current economic and political factors. In fact, such an interpretation has been strongly put forward. The deterioration of attitudes toward work is seen by many commentators as part of a broad decline in bourgeois values—the esteem for independence, responsibility, and respectability.[6]

According to this change-of-values thesis, the successive generations have grown up under markedly different conditions, and the changes have led to changes in values. The generations making up the labor force in the postwar years up to the mid-1960s had known hardships. Those of us in the Silent Generation, now in our fifties and sixties, were raised in the Great Depression and World War II so we became accustomed to a certain amount of deprivation and delay of gratification.[7] And few of our mothers were in the labor force, so there was someone home to make sure we did our homework. Thus we grew up prepared to make the sacrifices needed to make something of ourselves. (We were put off by social conformity and the company man, but our response was to go more into the professions or small businesses, not to rebel against bourgeois values.) The Me Generation of baby boomers, born between 1946 and the mid-1960s and streaming into the labor force from the mid-1960s until the mid-1980s, did not go through such chastening hardships. The subsequent Generation X saw their parents endowed with a range of social protections and their grandparents cushioned against poverty by the welfare state—though skepticism about the permanence of these entitlements is setting in.

But recent experience does not offer clear evidence of the *importance* of the decline of bourgeois values for the decline of work. Consider the unemployment record. In Italy, where bourgeois values seem pretty much intact, we find the second-largest fall of employment in the West in recent decades. (The largest decline was in Spain, which could serve as another example.) In fact, experts suggest that Italian unemployment would have risen *less* had the sense of family obligation not been so strong. Unemployed youth in the Mezzogiorno, rather than being pushed out of the nest to find jobs in the north, were welcome to live at home until such time as a job in the public sector could be arranged. Consider next the wage record. The largest declines in the relative wage of the low-paid over the past two decades have occurred in America, Great Britain, and Canada. But are these the western countries where morals have declined most?

It would be hasty to conclude that the effects of such cultural changes as have occurred in the past generation or two have been absent or weak. Yet international postwar evidence suggests that *economic* changes have been powerful—though some part of their power surely lies in the attitudinal changes that follow in their wake. If the welfare state works its ill effects partly by corroding values, so independence is less prized and responsibility for self and others less strongly felt, it is natural to call the welfare state the cause and the corrosion of values an intermediate effect—and not necessarily irreversible.

Racial History

It has been cited as a "killer fact" that of the Standard Metropolitan Areas in which the majority are classified as poor, not one is predominantly white.[8] It is a commonplace that the incidence of low wages and of joblessness is considerably higher among blacks and, to a somewhat lesser extent, Hispanics, than among whites. In 1973, a year of normal tightness in the labor market, the general unemployment rate was not quite 5 percent while the unemployment rate among blacks was 9½ percent. In 1994, again a normal year though by this time the normal level had crept up considerably, the general unemployment rate was around 6 percent while that among blacks was around 10½ percent. Among men aged 20 and over, the white rate went from 3 percent to 5 percent over the same period, while the black rate went from 6 percent to about 10 percent—neatly maintaining the historical ratio of two to one. Wage rates also show black-white differences, more pronounced for men than for women.

Among men these wage differences have widened over the past generation. Black male high school graduates saw a larger decline of their relative wage in the past two decades (some 22½ percent) than high school graduates as a whole, and black male high school dropouts suffered a larger decline of their relative wage (nearly 47½ percent).[9]

Some say that the roots of these longstanding disparities lie in racial history and will be hard to eradicate. In their view the history of blacks in this country has deposited a "black American culture" and this distinctive culture is somehow a cause of low employment and wages among American blacks and, therefore, of the exceptional scale and depth of economic disadvantage in this country. (A distinctive Hispanic-American culture is obviously traced to other origins.) Something in the perceptions and values of black communities, it is felt, fosters underdevelopment, manifested in low productivity and low wages, which (in the context of a rich country) leads in turn to poor job attachment and job performance, and thus to high unemployment.

Of course history matters, but not necessarily by creating a mutant culture. There are ways in which any low-wage group within the population that is squeezed involuntarily into large and dense concentrations is disadvantaged by the segregation—regardless of race. With the decline of agriculture, blacks and Hispanics, most of them having little or no wealth, were the ones driven into low-rent areas of the inner city, while disadvantaged white wage earners remained more dispersed, using their greater wealth to stay in their rural areas or to buy into low-density urban areas.

A second historical factor affects blacks, though again one not unique to their race. Poor blacks have been here a long time and so many have accumulated significant assets, from houses and cars to stores and other property. They also may draw upon a substantial stock of social wealth in various contingencies; many know the ins and outs of access to those entitlements and have networks of friends and relatives on whom they can depend for economic support when the need arises. By contrast, immigrants with the same level of education do not have all this access to support and so must rely on their own earning power. It is also said that immigrants who are illegal are reluctant to make trouble over factory safety or other employer abuses for fear of being turned in and sent home, while native-born blacks have no reason to be so compliant.

The standard cultural thesis speaks of blacks as molded by their unique racial history in this country. Under slavery, it is argued, blacks generally lacked the reward structure that would have encouraged them to develop habits of industry and thrift, and they lacked the investment opportunities that would have let them develop commercial expertise. The racial tensions of the Reconstruction era continued to discourage blacks from efforts to better their economic position. Finally, it is suggested, American blacks were less often brought up to take pleasure in learning, their roots being farther from the high culture of Europe than those of the white immigrants and their descendants. Thus there has arisen, according to this thesis, a distinct black culture in America that fails to nourish an active commercial economy and a high level of economic development.[10]

Does this thesis help explain the sharp decline in the wages and employment of the poorer blacks over the past two decades? If this black culture exists and is dysfunctional, it could have made blacks particularly vulnerable to economic shocks that struck all low-wage workers over the past two decades. If so, a distinctive black culture—even though not something rising up out of nowhere in 1975 or so—could be a factor in both the low level of black earnings before the 1970s and the sharp relative deterioration since then.

The prevalence of such a distinct outlook is a matter of some debate, though. It is true that black American communities have started fewer businesses relative to their numbers than have the Asian emigrant communities both in America and elsewhere (the Koreans and Vietnamese in the United States, the Chinese in Hong Kong, and the Indians in East Africa). There is also hard evidence that children growing up in homes where the parents have little human capital, as has been the case relatively often among black families in America, tend themselves to acquire little such capital.[11]

But where are the signs that there is a *different* economic culture among black Americans? Black and Hispanic ghettos do not lack for entrepreneurs if we count those operating in the underground economy, including illegal businesses. (As Peter Davis notes, the question is why the entrepreneurs on ghetto streets seem to be primarily drug dealers.)[12] In a speech to the Manhattan Institute, Tom Wolfe, fresh from the success of his novel *Bonfire of the Vanities,* found in black entrepreneurs some of the same ambitions and tastes displayed by a great many white financiers and businessmen. Black Americans, having lived under America's individualism for generations, appear to accept that individualism, not the communitarianism and socialism of some African nations—though the dearth of opportunities has often thrown them back on community and state for support. They appear also to embrace the ideal of positions based on merit—complaining only that this ideal is not the reality. The differences in the scale and form of their entrepreneurship, and in their ways of making money generally, may be attributable mainly to differences in opportunity.

Observations like these suggest a less radical position. The cultural handicap of the disadvantaged among blacks and Hispanics is not that they have a *different* economic culture but that they have had *less access* to bourgeois business culture. When parents can gain only limited experience in business, their children lack an important window to the values and possibilities of that world. And when parents and neighbors have little education they are unable to help with their children's schooling and less likely to encourage them to seek more education. Thus people growing up in poor communities generally gain less knowledge of business life than people growing up elsewhere. They can progress, however. (In this century we have seen the Irish and the Italians catch up.) Studies of the speed with which groups and nations progress from generation to generation do not give promise that every group will catch up entirely; there may be some permanent component holding a group back—some economic disadvantage that the culture persists in transmitting.

Even if a difference in culture *is* an enduring component among American blacks, it does not necessarily explain much of the difference in wage rates and unemployment rates between blacks and whites. Furthermore, the presence of stubborn factors exerting a drag on the prosperity of blacks and Hispanics, even if these factors were irreducible forever, would not mean that a government program to pull up wage rates and employment at the bottom would *fail* with respect to blacks and Hispanics.

Racial Discrimination

It continues to be maintained that blacks, Hispanics, and to varying degrees other ethnic groups meet discrimination and that it results in lower wages and depressed employment. Discrimination, according to this view, is the short answer to why blacks and Hispanics figure disproportionately among the disadvantaged. And that is why the problem of economic disadvantage is so much deeper and broader in this country than in other advanced economies of the West, since blacks and Hispanics make up a much larger proportion of the population here.

Classic discrimination springs from fear of what is foreign—a different skin color or language or dress or religious practice. It may wear off as the foreign becomes familiar. Anti-Catholicism died down in this country once it was demonstrated that Roman Catholics were not under the control of a foreign power, and anti-Semitism receded as Jews pursued assimilation. Likewise it is difficult to believe that whites' uneasiness with blacks' skin color is any longer a large damper on blacks' rewards from working, investing, and marketing—not after the integration of the armed forces and colleges and the considerable integration of so many enterprises in the cities over the past half-century. The rise of a substantial black bourgeoisie in recent decades is strong evidence against that.

Today, blacks and perhaps to a lesser extent Hispanics face prejudice based more commonly on their behavior rather than their color. Employers, lenders, and buyers, it is generally conceded, distrust the ghetto teenagers emerging from the disadvantaged neighborhoods of the inner city. In more concrete terms, employers (black or white) have correctly estimated the behavior of these disadvantaged job applicants and, to avoid the costs of the consequent low job attachment and unreliable job performance, have opted to hire others instead. This is "rational discrimination," to use a recent term for it.[13] But it is not discrimination in the more usual sense of the word, in which some persons have *limited* information used against them, which may strike us as extremely unfair.

A kind of discrimination that seems unfair is statistical discrimination. This came up earlier, where it was noted that even a person's address may count in a job application; then persons from certain neighborhoods suffer reduced wages and, as a by-product, reduced employment as well. In this view of things it is quite possible that a job applicant's being a black American will count against him or her. If the employer knows little else about the applicant, and if the employer believes—correctly, in the simple version of the theory—that relatively fewer blacks make reliable and loyal employees, the employer may reject the applicant on racial grounds alone. Thus even those applicants who would perform well may be undeservedly rejected. Conceivably everyone will persevere despite early disappointments and the best employees will be filtered through to successful careers. But in more realistic scenarios, a person who expects to be unable to make it to a level where high or medium skills would be valuable has a reason not to invest in acquiring those skills. As a result, according to this view, fewer people in the black community will make it to the rung in the ladder that they would have reached had their race not worked against them in the early sorting process.

In all this we should bear in mind that presumably the unfavorable behavior did not come out of the blue. Undoubtedly it arose to a very large extent as a defensive reaction to the failure to gain acceptance in the earlier days, when race was an issue, and, even worse, the later failure to do well when the rules became fairer. Hence improvements in economic conditions will serve to send these values into decline. And even if not, there is much that economic policy can do to improve the situation of the disadvantaged, black as well as white.

Of course there are cultural influences. But their share of the blame for the severity of economic disadvantage in this country and for its worsening in recent decades is not easy to ascertain. It may be granted that individuals who, though not themselves disadvantaged, have the statistical earmarks of belonging to a disadvantaged group are burdened by the group's poor reputation; and they may underinvest in themselves in anticipation of this prejudice; so fewer of them rise up the ladder than otherwise would. But maybe this is not culture. It may also be granted that some disadvantaged groups are being held back by their adverse history, which creates a kind of culture of poverty that acts as a drag on their economic development. But their century-long past cannot apparently explain why the relative wages of some of the disadvantaged plummeted over the space of a decade and their unemployment rose sharply. Finally, it may be conceded that the values of today's younger generations were shaped differently from those of the children of the Depression, let alone the children of Victorian times. But among the advanced economies in recent decades, every one, no matter what its culture, has sooner or later felt downward pressure on wages or employment or both, especially among its less advantaged members.

Even if culture were quite important, to go from that to the ineffectiveness of economic policy would be unwarranted. Government action to reward firms for their employment of low-wage workers, for example—the plan I argue for in this book—in raising the wage that the employer can afford to pay these workers would raise wage rates of all the disadvantaged, blacks, Hispanics, and every other group. If their performance as employees did not respond, that wage increase would be the whole of the improvement in their position—no mean achievement in itself. But their performance surely would improve as they recognized the higher rewards from finding and holding a job.

The battle against this same pessimistic mind-set is going on in Eastern Europe. The debate over whether blacks and Hispanics are "different" parallels the dispute between the Sovietologists who say that the Russians and other peoples far to the east are different, lacking the predisposition or background needed for prospering in a market economy, and the reform economists who say there is no reason to suppose any such thing.[14]

The cultural approach to the cause and cure of poverty goes too far in treating social attitudes, such as that toward work, as if they were either impervious to economic and political factors or a sort of non-biodegradable sludge left by the worst such factors in the past that no economic program could dissolve. As the philosopher Richard Rorty put it, "there will always be a civilization gap between people with hope and people without it, people who know they have a chance in life and people who know they don't."[15]

6

·

Economic Sources

Economic factors create substantial gaps between the wage rates in the lower reaches of the distribution and, to take a meaningful reference point, the median wage. Where the gap is large, of course, many with low wage prospects are stimulated to improve their qualifications, through additional education for example, to gain a higher wage; but the additional education induced does not proceed far enough to eliminate these gaps, pulling everyone up to the median wage, since education is costly and onerous to students. When economic forces widen the gap, further education is stimulated; but the gap is not narrowed to its previous size. (The cost of the extra education required to earn the median wage increases as the ranks of the less educated thin.)

The intensification of some of these economic forces in the past two decades provides a rough explanation for most of the widening of wage gaps. These forces also help to explain the marked widening of the gap in joblessness between workers of average education and the less educated. Identifying these causes is important for our thinking about the nation's economic policy, since it matters whether the causes are permanent or transitory or only the beginning.

Relative Productivity and Relative Wages

Why are some people's wages so low? The answer is largely that their productivity in their place of employment is low—low in the job that makes the best use of them, that is. (Every one of them might be highly effective at running the company, but some of them only at the cost of displacing someone else so much more productive in that position that output would be reduced.) A worker's private productivity is what his or her contribution is worth to the employer. Employers, in their competition for workers, find themselves ultimately paying each worker a wage equal to what they estimate the worker's productivity to be.

Of course a worker's productivity is to some extent a matter of circumstances, not an attribute inherent in the worker. Plop an Iowa worker into another world economy somewhere in the cosmos and his or her productivity might be wildly higher or lower. Yet, to come back to this world, an Iowan's productivity does not depend very much on the sheer number of Iowa workers in the world nor the number like him or her.[1] A sharp increase in the number of these Iowans would cause congestion (hence diminishing returns) in the short run but not in the long run when capital facilities would catch up.

Analogously, the productivity of American workers who are high-school dropouts, for example, is not very sensitive to how many American dropouts there are in the world. (There are so many other workers like them linked to the global economy that the American ones are too few for their relative numbers to matter much; furthermore, if the number of dropouts decreased worldwide, employers could turn to high school graduates as substitutes.) This is a point of some substantive importance, for it implies that increased numbers completing high school, say, will not depress the wage of high school graduates by much (the good news) but also will do little to raise the wage of the remaining dropouts (the bad news). It implies that the number of low-wage workers below a given wage is not finally a result of immigration or other supply factors but simply the number who lack the talent or training or whatever else it takes to qualify for high- or middle-productivity jobs.

Three prominent theses tie the decline in relative wages of the less productive to a decline in their relative productivity. These theses concern information and learning to learn, import competition, and interest rates.

Information and Learning to Learn

What is it, exactly, that workers are productive *at?* It has become standard to speak of three stages in the character of production: the commodity-processing era ushered in by the railways, the era of electricity-powered mass manufacturing, and now the age of information technology, driven by computers and semiconductors.[2] In fact, there has always been a layer of any enterprise's workforce heavily occupied with information processing. The managers of farms, mines, and firms in the manufacturing and services sectors must gather and process information about available production techniques, available financing, personnel, customers, and markets. Yet there is no doubt that, on the whole, production is less and less about handling objects and more and more about handling information.

A worker's productivity in a job, then, is today largely a matter of the volume and the value of the information to be gathered or processed or transmitted. In a dynamic economy, such as ours has proved to be, an enterprise's profitability and survival depend on keeping abreast of new technologies and new markets and investing accordingly. At small enterprises this is a primary function of the manager—the farmer poring over the new seed catalog, the winegrower studying the latest insecticides—and it may take much of his time. At large enterprises a major part of the workforce may be occupied with information: not only the research department but also the marketing, personnel, and finance departments. On some criteria, some 70 percent of the employees of the Xerox Corporation are information workers.

There have been enormous advances in communication and

computation over recent decades that have greatly increased the information-handling capacity of employees in a range of positions. Clearly the upper and middle levels of management operate today with far wider information than could have been imagined even a few decades ago.

What has the new information age meant for the relative productivity of workers in the lower parts of the wage distribution? Two forces creating a gap between wages toward the bottom and wages in the middle can be identified. First, the new age has been a boon for those with talent and skill at information handling. When productivity and hence wages were more governed than they are now by quickness, concentration, strength, and endurance as well as attractiveness, drive, and physical and emotional health, there was less room for large percentage differences in productivity and wages. (People who could pick half as much fruit or make half as many egg rolls as the median worker could earn half the median wage.) The new importance of various cognitive abilities—memory, detecting patterns, reasoning power, and knowledge of various tools of analysis—has opened up another dimension on which people may differ quite a lot. To the extent that information-processing ability, like the other attributes, is distributed unequally across the labor force and more or less independently of the way the other attributes are distributed, this newly important source of disparities adds to the dispersion in wage rates. Differences in people's natural powers of memory and analysis play a part, of course, and so do differences in level of education attained.

The new premium on the ability to handle information goes some distance toward solving a puzzle. Since the early 1980s widening differences in earnings even among workers of the same age, sex, and years of schooling have been observed. The success of the so-called cybernerds and propeller-heads within such groups may be the explanation of these disparities.

The role of education points to another channel through which the increased importance of information widens wage gaps. Education, in the standard view, is learning how to learn, to grasp terminologies and use logic. Accordingly, what is called the Nelson-Phelps thesis posits that people's broad education helps equip them to acquire and grasp new or unfamiliar information in various fields during their careers—data on new technology and equipment, on unfamiliar markets, new legislation, or procedures at an unfamiliar firm.[3] Thus the less educated are apt not to be selected for jobs requiring adaptation to new information. Since the low-paid are less educated on the whole, the flow of new technical information widens the gap between low-wage and median-wage workers. (A plausible measure of the increased difficulty of keeping abreast of technological changes can be obtained by charting the expenditures on research and development. Since the late 1970s these scientific and engineering outlays have spurted ahead—though it is uncertain whether the pace of technical progress has picked up in response. The 1980s were disappointing in this respect, but the 1990s have been a great deal better.)

This thesis applies also to workers' capacity to grasp the information a firm gives trainees. Although workers generally come to their employer having provided for their own vocational training and any higher education, the employer typically needs to give new recruits training that they cannot have gotten elsewhere—training specific to the firm. To become a functioning employee, a worker will need to become familiar with the objectives, operations, and personnel that are specific to the firm.

For any given job, the training that the employer will find appropriate to give a worker will be more costly (if feasible at all) the less the worker's schooling and the greater the job's complexity. When, in the information revolution, some jobs previously held by workers with low education become more complex, employers find it unprofitable to hire these workers, because the training costs would be too high to be repaid by the resulting gain in productivity. As the training requirements of new workers rise with increased specialization and sophistication of jobs at a given firm, the workers who would have been hired previously may be shunted down to other firms where they can function with less costly training but where they will have lower productivity. In this view, the increased sophistication of jobs has operated to reduce sharply the net productivity of the less educated workers when allowance is made for the increased training burden that those workers pose for potential employers.[4] (It is not necessary to suppose that high schools deliver reduced education.)

Evidence exists in support of this line of thinking. It has been found that costs of production are greater where workers are less educated or less trained.[5] And now there are findings that countries where education is higher are better at catching up or staying close to the world technological leader.[6] What applies to countries applies also to communities. In those communities where education is low, the gap between productivity there and productivity at the leading edge will widen until it reaches a point where, despite the low education, the rate of learning, though low, is enough to prevent the gap from widening further.

A case in point has been discussed by the English economist Stephen Nickell. The country that wins the prize for its secondary education, which is nearly universal and very serious, is surely the former West Germany. It is also the only nation in the OECD to avoid a fall in the relative pay of those in the bottom parts of the wage distribution. (And it does this with only a modest rise in the relative unemployment rate of the less educated, which suggests that trade unions or the welfare state were not a factor here, blocking wage cuts that would have matched productivity declines and thus damaging employment.) Nickell proposes a connection. Few in Germany are confined to low-skill work, so what happens to *its* economic value has little effect on wages even in the lowest reaches of the distribution. From the perspective of the thesis here, these workers' education gives them the versatility to adapt to the new technologies with little reduction in their productivity relative to that of the others in the labor force.[7]

Thinking about education kindles hopes that it holds an effective solution to the problem of the disadvantaged in America. Possibly we would do well to duplicate Germany's education here, despite its great cost. But, first, it would take us decades to build it. Second, even if we could have it tomorrow, it would not raise the prospects of workers whose secondary education is behind them. And, third, what exactly is Germany's system? It is an admixture of abstract education and applied instruction leading to apprenticeship. Possibly the latter works the wrong way by diverting too soon the students taking that path to particular skills at the expense of further general education. If we venture this way, it will be a voyage into the unknown.

The information economy also influences wage differentials through its effect on the interpersonal aspect of jobs. In the classic factories, manufacturing workers did not have much interchange with clients or suppliers or even with one another. In contrast, much of information transmission is interpersonal, needing to be done face to face or over the telephone—consulting with colleagues, advising customers, inquiring at suppliers, and so forth. Women are said generally to be more adroit than men at this work, much of which is performed in the service industries. As the importance of information grows, this gender difference may be another factor narrowing the gap between the wage of women and that of men.

There is, finally, a second force driving a wedge between low- and middle-level wages. A great number of the technical advances in recent decades have introduced equipment that automated the information processing formerly done by workers—by telephone receptionists, bank tellers, and clerks of all kinds. ("Press 1 if you want . . .") These innovations are strongly labor-saving, operating to reduce rather than to raise wages—some wages, at any rate. If a technical improvement opens the way to new machinery that can perform for $5 an hour the manufacturing tasks that unskilled workers were doing at a higher hourly wage, their wage must eventually drop to $5.[8]

This has not always been the effect of new machinery. The introduction of equipment organized for an assembly line appears to have been only mildly labor-saving, if labor-saving at all—as the rewards to labor were pulled up, though not necessarily as much as the returns to capital. It is difficult to see in the new generation of machinery, however, anything but a tendency to use machines to process a great deal of information that formerly required labor.

Import Competition

The most hotly disputed new thesis on the decline of low-wage labor blames it on new sources of foreign competition. Since the late 1970s, this thesis notes, the emerging market economies of Asia have made big inroads into the world market for a range of mass-production manufactures, such as textiles, autos, and electronics—goods that we used to import but also produced ourselves. The foreign suppliers, in winning an increased market share, have forced major cutbacks in American output of these goods. The workers losing their jobs, if not to remain unemployed or leave the labor force, have been forced to find jobs in the service industries or in other manufacturing industries. Further, the thesis goes, the manufacturing industries hit by imports generally make intensive use of *less educated* labor (using large doses of "production workers" on the assembly line or shop floor relative to other inputs), while the production of services is generally intensive in *more educated* labor; and the latter tends also to be true of the other industries in manufacturing to which the less educated may go. As a result, the less educated have found themselves initially in surplus: they have had to accept a lower wage in order to crowd into services or other manufacturing (where there was little accompanying inflow of skilled labor) or accept unemployment or leave the labor force—or a combination of all three. This is the popular thesis.[9]

The economists' version of this thesis brings price into the picture. In this view, wages are ultimately governed by economic productivity, and this productivity is not purely physical. A worker's economic productivity in an activity is the contribution to physical output valued at the relative price of that product. (The output contributed is multiplied by the relative price.) The rush of foreign imports takes away market share by driving down the price of these manufactures relative to the prices of services and of other manufactures. This in turn reduces the real wage that the manufacturers can afford to pay their less educated employees; it reduces the economic productivity of the less educated workers in manufacturing. Since that is the sector in which they are important, there is ultimately a fall in their economy-wide wage. (The drop in their productivity implied by the fall in the relative price of the affected manufactures, where less educated labor is relatively important, outweighs the rise in their productivity provided by the rise in the relative price of services or other manufactures.) In a mirror-opposite process, educated labor ends up with an increased wage.

The early quantitative evidence for this thesis has been circumstantial. In the first three postwar decades jobs in manufacturing fell only a little relative to aggregate employment, and from the late 1970s to the early 1990s manufacturing jobs contracted sharply, both relative to the aggregate and in absolute terms. Correspondingly, our imports of manufactures relative to our domestic output, which had been rising moderately in the earlier period, rose steeply in the 1970s and 1980s. The increase in imports has also been examined industry by industry to see how much displacement of skilled workers and unskilled workers these increases could hypothetically account for (based on the assumption that each imported unit of a manufacture means one less unit produced domestically).[10] Such calculations put the resulting job cuts at between 5 and 6 percent of the manufacturing total. These job cuts were somewhat deeper (about 6 percent) among production workers, who are generally less educated and lower paid, than among nonproduction workers (about 4 percent).[11]

The champions of free trade (a great majority of the trade economists in this country) have been rattled by these findings. They had not presented to the public the classical case for free trade as it really is—a story about losers from free trade as well as gainers in which the gainers could compensate the losers and still come out ahead (theoretically at any rate). They had assumed as a practical matter that the losses from free trade were small enough to be ignored (as perhaps they were in earlier times). However, the shakiness of this evidence has given the defenders of free trade ample grounds for a rebuttal.

The job displacement studies, the critics say, do not show that import competition is even a major factor in the decline of the unskilled worker, let alone the primary factor.[12] For one thing, the job loss of the unskilled relative to that of the skilled in manufacturing looks to be small potatoes. And manufacturing, about one-sixth of nonagricultural employment in this country, is so small that the recent acceleration of its decline cannot affect wage differentials very much. Imports from the developing countries are simply too small to have a large impact on the wages of the unskilled. For another, it is a jump to go from job cuts, also known as the displacement of workers, to a decrease in their wage. Maybe the unskilled workers and their skilled co-workers displaced by imports have slipped into employment in other manufacturing industries—in industries that are just as unskilled-intensive as the ones they came from. (The unskilled have apparently not poured into services.[13] So where else can they have gone?) The upshot is that we do not know that the workers who would have been hired in manufacturing but for increased imports did markedly worse in their next-best possibility. (The unskilled *are* doing worse than two decades ago, but the question is the part played by foreign trade.)

Then, going on the offensive, the critics propose a different way of getting at the magnitude of the wage cut that may have resulted from import competition: looking at how much the average relative price of goods whose manufacture is intensive in less educated workers fell. Several economists have pored over the price data and found little or no such fall. (The average price of all manufactures relative to that of all services did fall markedly in the two decades between the mid-1970s and the mid-1990s but no faster than during the two previous decades. Investigators looking at price changes within manufacturing were surprised to find that relative declines were not concentrated in industries where workers were least skilled.)[14] More recent work, though, has found that in the 1990s the larger price declines in manufacturing have been in those industries making the most intensive use of less skilled workers.[15] Yet this decline is not nearly great enough nor is the manufacturing sector big enough to explain more than a small fraction of the relative decline of unskilled wages.

Some of the critics also argue that if the newly emerging market economies were such a big factor in America they would also have had large effects on relative wages and relative unemployment rates in other advanced economies. Yet we do not observe such a pattern on the European continent.[16]

Nevertheless, the critics' counterarguments could be insufficient to win their case. If few unskilled workers have moved from import-competing manufacturing to other industries, it may be that large numbers of them have instead gone into unemployment or left the labor force. The wage has no necessary tendency to fall by enough to make room for all of them in other industries. Such a tendency toward a semblance of rigidity in real wages would also lead us to expect that increased competition from imports would have less of an effect on relative prices and real wages than on outputs and employment.[17] Data on unemployment rates by education show that the ratio of the low-education unemployment rate to the middle-education unemployment rate has steadily risen. Also, while it is true that on some measures over some short time periods (especially beginning in 1982) the ratio of blue-collar unemployment to white-collar unemployment has been falling, it has a long way to go to fall to its level of the mid-1970s.[18]

Furthermore, the critics' view that American trade with developing economies is too small to matter much is cold comfort since this trade is bound to grow. Optimists take heart in the point that as the emerging economies develop the education of their workforces will improve, reducing their competition with our less educated labor and increasing their competition with our educated labor instead. But there are whole continents of less developed countries with the potential to emerge as factors in the global economy. It is likely that developing countries will penetrate the global market faster than formerly developing nations will graduate to developed status. So the pressure coming from the developing world on the gap between low wages and median wages is likely to get worse before it gets better.

Moreover, other channels have been conceived through which our openness to world markets may have reduced domestic wage rates, especially at the low end. One such channel is the globalization of goods markets. It is thought to have exposed domestic producers to greater risks, such as a drain of customers or an increase of interest costs. In general, increased risks of doing business make producers think twice before investing in new employees or even old employees. Thus workers' productivity as risk-shy employers evaluate it would be judged to have fallen, pushing down wages (both relative to trend). It is a good guess that such a hesitancy to invest in employees would hit hardest those job applicants who are considered the most risky, who are the low-wage workers, generally speaking, since they do not have many credentials in the way of test scores and hurdles jumped in arriving at their present qualifications. (The French speak ominously of workers *sans qualification*.) However, it would surely hit the more credentialed applicants as well, even employees of substantial experience within the firm. This may be the explanation of downsizing within the ranks of middle management in spite of currently profitable conditions.

Another such channel is the globalization of the capital market, including the greater hospitality to direct foreign investment in a great many countries. It is argued that, with national capital free to skip overseas, unions have seen employers threatening to move operations overseas, which has forced unions to accept poorer wage bargains. In fact, such a development is better able to explain the decline of wages among middle-wage workers than among low-wage workers. In any case, unions are continuing to shrink as a factor in wage setting in this country. But the argument could be seen as an explanation of the marked decline of unions in recent decades alongside a decline in wages relative to productivity.

Interest Rates

The rise of interest rates in the global capital market is another factor operating to reduce workers' net productivity—and, very likely, to reduce that of low-wage employees more than that of middle-wage employees. In the early 1980s, when less than half of the widening of the gap between low and median wages had occurred, long-term interest rates were driven up to a new plateau at which they have more or less held for the past decade and a half. (The reference here is to real interest rates—rates obtained after netting out the rate of inflation.) At first this increase in capital costs seemed to be more the result of various fiscal stimuli enacted by the U.S. Congress than of any sea change in the world economy. But most of these fiscal stimuli were later retracted, while the rise in interest rates persisted, though not at the extraordinary heights of the mid-1980s. Most students of interest rates are prepared to assign much of the continuing elevation to the high rates of return to investment that global investors foresee in the emerging market economies.

One of the ways by which the interest rate affects a worker's net productivity is through the on-the-job training phenomenon discussed earlier. When the firm trains a new employee, thus making an investment in the worker, the annual interest on that investment must be deducted from the worker's annual contribution to revenues to get the worker's net productivity. Thus in the early 1980s when long-term interest rates rose, the interest component of the employer's allowance for training costs increased correspondingly. Since the prospective annual interest cost of new employees would be higher as a result, new employees would not be able to command as high a wage as those employees whose training had been financed at a lower interest rate.[19]

An increase in interest rates will widen the percentage gap between low wages and the median wage provided that training cost is generally a larger consideration in the hiring of low-wage workers than in the hiring of more advantaged workers. Some do not go along with that proviso. But one thing is clear. The presence of low-wage jobs in which the employer's training costs are negligible is not evidence against the proposition that workers of relatively low education were bumped down to such jobs because, with interest rates much higher, they were no longer deemed good investments in the higher-rung jobs they once occupied. And what counts for the percentage wage impact of increased interest rates is training cost *relative* to the wage.

The interest rate figures much more widely in wages. There is a whole class of other ways by which an outlay for labor in the present makes its contribution to revenues only in the future. Much of an employee's productive effort contributes to revenues in the future rather than to the present. Mankind plants trees, Cicero said quoting Caecilius Statius, to benefit future generations. Classical economics (not as classical as Statius) has always recognized that the input of labor today comes to fruition in output months or years later.

The beloved classical example is indeed trees. After a lumber producer lays out wages to plant a tree, the seedling will grow and will be cut down when its wood is no longer growing fast enough to justify waiting longer. In the classical theory, competition in the lumber industry will pull up the wage to a level that reflects what the prospect of that *future* tree is worth in the *present*—which means discounting that future value by the interest rate to get its present value. Clearly an increase of interest rates reduces such present values. Hence an increase of interest rates, by causing such future values to be discounted more heavily, brings about an immediate drop in what producers of lumber are willing to pay for labor. And it is not just growing things. An increase of interest rates puts downward pressure on the prices of all manner of capital goods, from structures to equipment. If we still build residential and commercial buildings largely the way the Babylonians did, that is, in a relatively labor-intensive way, a drop in the price of these capital goods (and other capital goods that are relatively labor-intensive) will put downward pressure on wage rates.

There is a more modern example of the future payoff of present labor. Firms, in a contemporary view, do not sell in a perfectly frictionless auction-type market; they sell to accumulated customers who will not vanish instantaneously at the sight of a small price increase. (The customers may scurry around in confusion, but they will not all be able to locate satisfactory alternative suppliers immediately, if only because many of them will be poorly informed and too busy to become informed right away.) Thus each firm possesses a degree of monopoly power—at least in the short run. But firms do not set their mark-up as high as would be in their short-term interest to do. They temper their mark-up in view of their long-term interest in having customers to sell to in the future. If interest rates rise, this long-run interest is given less weight compared to near-term interests. That means an increase of the mark-up—behavior more like that of a monopolist. And that means lower wage rates—since pushing up prices relative to the money wage pulls down the wage. (The wage here always means the wage relative to the price level, that is, the wage adjusted for inflation, called the real wage.)

Once again it may be asked how this affects the disparities in wage rates. Is there any presumption that an increase of the rate of interest reduces low wage rates proportionately more than it reduces high wage rates? It is plausible that workers with low education need more training relative to their wage than workers with more education, so we could argue that a higher interest rate would hit the low-wage worker harder. (Is it plausible that low-wage workers need more—relative to the wage—of *all* the various kinds of capital considered here? Maybe so. Perhaps secretaries receiving one-tenth the wage of the company president receive more than one-tenth of his floor space and far more than one-tenth of his equipment.)

Suppose, though, that there is no such greater capital intensiveness among low-wage workers. Even then we have gained something: the historic rise of interest rates is another factor operating to reduce the wages of the disadvantaged; and although a similar reduction in high wages is also implied, which did not happen, there are other factors capable of explaining the rise in the upper wages—the sharp increase in the gains from trade and, perhaps, the information revolution. Thus, even if the interest rate taken alone operates to reduce all wages equally, it helps to explain why wages toward the bottom of the distribution went down when until recently it was thought that wages could only go up.

Relative Productivity and the Unemployment Rate Spread

The widened gap, or ratio, between the pay of low-wage workers and those in the middle has been accompanied by a widened spread, or difference, between their unemployment rates. As noted earlier, the increase in the spread is part of the deterioration in the situation of the disadvantaged in recent decades.

To understand how an adverse shock might operate to increase unemployment, and how policy remedies operate to reduce that unemployment, we need to understand a few basic ideas about why unemployment is normal in a market economy—why the "natural" unemployment rate is substantial. There are many reasons. Some workers are in motion, heading for a new locale in search of a better wage or working conditions. Other workers are between jobs yet motionless, waiting for the phone to ring with the next contract. Beyond these two classical types of unemployment, called frictional, are some more modern forms of joblessness. Labor union power may block unemployed workers from gaining a unionized job. So may pressure from a firm's insiders, who see the hiring of cheaper labor as the camel's nose in the tent. Established firms intent on keeping their personnel may give priority to the job security of their existing employees.

The usual perspective on wages and unemployment is centered around the phenomenon generally known as the incentive wage. Employers, in the interest of the efficiency of their operations, keep their wages high, too high to permit all in the labor force to be employed at the same time. All employers understand that they must overpay workers—pay them more than they require to give up the leisure time—in order to give them adequate incentives to stay on and perform well. Each employer calculates the amount to overpay, bearing in mind how much the other employers are paying and how high is the unemployment that awaits an employee who quits or performs badly. When jobless workers appear at the factory gate to offer their services for a lower wage, therefore, the employer will refuse, even if persuaded that they are identical in their capacities to the workers currently employed.

The employer understands that the saving in wages per hour would be more than offset by the increase in costs caused by the lower reliability and poorer performance that the lower wage would invite.

How large, on this view, does the unemployment pool tend to be? Just large enough to reconcile the wage required by incentive considerations—call it the required wage—with the wage level that employers could afford to go on paying their workforce and make a normal return on their investment—call it the affordable wage. If unemployment is quite low to start with, for example, the required wage in such tight labor-market conditions will *exceed* the affordable wage. So employers will start cutting back their workforce, perhaps by ceasing for a time to replace employees who retire or quit. Thus the amount of unemployment will rise. It must go on rising until this swelling of joblessness, in exerting discipline on employees, finally lowers the required wage to the level of the affordable wage.

If technological shocks, say, decrease affordable wages but not required wages (or at least not as much), the effect must be a decline of market wages *and* a decline of employment—a rise of unemployment and whatever shrinkage of the labor force also results. Unemployment must rise because the required incentive wages do not absorb the shocks. With private and social wealth initially unchanged, employee performance and attachment will be initially unchanged. So the required incentive wage does not accommodate the decline in the wage that employers can afford to go on paying their workforce. Hence employment must fall. Though performance and attachment then improve, it is only because unemployment has gone up; this in turn reduces the required incentive wages but not so as to eliminate the increased unemployment.

In the long run, as households run down their asset holdings to realign their wealth to their reduced wage, the unemployment rate tends to decline in the direction of its original level (but not all the way back if the entitlements of the welfare state are still geared to the former wage levels).

What of the composition of unemployment as between low-productivity and high-productivity workers? The above perspective generates several propositions. One is that the low-wage workers, having little job satisfaction and many of them not much prospect of rising very far, have higher quit rates and so are the ones whose wages are more driven up by employers' considerations of incentives; hence their unemployment rates are the higher. (Promotions and demotions, instead of unemployment, serve to discipline those higher up the company roster.) A related proposition is that as high-productivity workers become ever more informed about their firm and accordingly more valuable, they can less and less afford to start over elsewhere; so their wages and unemployment rates are less and less inflated by incentive considerations. Another proposition is that firms set wages above what is needed to fill the jobs in order to attract some good recruits, hoping later to identify and shed the bad ones, but this is less needed at the upper end of the job scale, where applicants can signal their industriousness and ability with their educational attainments. And then there is the whole armamentarium of entitlements provided by the welfare state, which offer a cushion against the penalties that low-wage employees risk for poor job performance or attachment—but more on this in the next chapter.

However, one does not need a broad knowledge of the forces acting on the composition of unemployment to grasp two main points. First, technological or other shocks that lower the wage that firms can afford to pay the less educated workers (while *not* lowering the wage that firms can afford to pay the more-educated workers) have the further effect of increasing the unemployment rate among the less educated and thus widening the spread between that unemployment rate and the unemployment rate of the more educated. The reason is that if the affordable wage for the less educated workers before the shock was equal to the required wage, the fall of the affordable wage puts it *below* the required wage—for there is nothing inherent in the shock that will transform the workers into more devoted employees (at least not at an unchanged wage). So their unemployment rate must rise until the required wage has fallen to the new and reduced level of the affordable wage.

Second, even an equal percentage fall (relative to trend, possibly) in the affordable wages of *all* workers tends to generate a larger increase of unemployment at the low end. One mechanism here is called bumping. (Another is the welfare state.) Struck by such a uniform change in the demand for labor, the more educated have the advantage that when finding themselves unemployed they can qualify for jobs requiring less education while losing little opportunity to be available for employment in their accustomed sort of job. The high-educated thus suffer a smaller increase of unemployment than do the less educated, though the former will suffer an increase of *under*employment as some of them take jobs below their ability.

Both kinds of shocks have larger effects on unemployment in the short run than in the long run. Facing a lower wage rate and possibly the prospect of less steady employment as well, workers are apt to reduce their saving for retirement or other purposes. The ensuing slowdown in accumulation of assets will in turn whittle away at the workers' independence from their bosses. As a result, the required incentive wages at any given unemployment level will decline. Thus unemployment will tend to recede, as reduced wages serve to "price" workers back into jobs. But this is less true of low-wage workers, much of whose wealth consists of entitlements that the workers cannot run down.

The gratifying partial recovery of unemployment rates in the mid-1990s against a background of fifteen years of remarkably low saving rates suggests that some of this recovery is attributable to this downward adjustment of wealth. The scare put into workers by the much-publicized wave of corporate downsizing has also served to drive down the required level of incentive wages. Yet unemployment rates today remain well above the accustomed levels of the 1950s and 1960s, most markedly the unemployment rates of those who are disadvantaged as measured by low education.

7

.

The Role of the Welfare System

The low wages and joblessness among the disadvantaged would be serious enough had the government initiatives of the postwar period not taken place. Yet American social policy has to be counted as one of the more important sources of high unemployment among disadvantaged workers. It has almost certainly been a significant factor in the widening over the past generation of the wage gap between disadvantaged workers and those in the middle.

The classical economic liberals, from Adam Smith to John Stuart Mill and John Maynard Keynes, held that the function of government was, as Lincoln put it, to do those things the people cannot do for themselves. From this classic perspective government intervention may be seen as responding to three kinds of societal problems: inefficiencies, inequities, and insecurity.

Preventing Inefficiencies

The great bulk of government purchases of goods and services, much of the government's subsidies to private producers, and some of its regulatory activities, are aimed (or purport to be aimed) at correcting or circumventing what is called market failure—the allocative inefficiencies or limitations of free markets.[1] In this category are expenditures for defense, law enforcement, and education, subsidies for science and the postal system, and tax breaks for private activities deemed to be in the public interest.

The subsidies here are, in general, oddly small (though there are several subsidies below the surface in the form of tax credits). In an economy producing $7 trillion per year, only $62 billion was spent by the government on research and development in 1994 while private industry spent $111 billion for this purpose.[2] The much-decried subsidies to energy and agriculture called "corporate welfare" amount to only $4 billion annually.[3]

Note that the term "corporate welfare" is a misnomer: the welfare system provides entitlements, not subsidies. Entitlement payments are made to people in a certain condition, such as unemployment or disability; the recipient does not have to do anything in return for the payment. Subsidies are grants in return for producing or working. Only the agricultural subsidies, in paying farmers on condition they restrict acreage ("for not planting"), could be likened to welfare entitlements. But even these payments have always been contingent on *some* farming.

Does government expenditure aimed at inefficiencies serve also to narrow the spread between low and median wages? To narrow the gap between the unemployment rates of the disadvantaged and those in the middle? In the economics born of the Depression of the 1930s—Keynesian doctrine—the answer was a fervent yes. Economists, and then the public, came to believe that government expenditure, like anyone else's expenditure, serves to move people from unemployment into jobs; and this fall of unemployment is greatest (relative to their number) among those whose unemployment was highest—low-wage workers.[4] Thus disadvantaged workers were held to be the main beneficiaries of government spending.

But beginning in the late 1960s, economists shifted from Keynesian doctrine to the notion of a natural unemployment rate—a rate to which the unemployment rate will tend unless government "demand management" repeatedly injects surprise doses of monetary or spending stimulus. (On this view, when the government hires a million workers or buys something from the private sector requiring as many, that is an increase of employment, all right; but if the unemployment rate cannot be below its natural level without causing the inflation rate to quicken year after year and that natural level is not appreciably affected by the government's action, this increased employment has to be counterbalanced sooner or later by a decrease of employment somewhere else in the economy.) And when the public was no longer asked to take on faith the Keynesian claims, popular support for them dwindled. The survey researcher Daniel Yankelovitch reported on the basis of his opinion polls that once the public gathered that their jobs did not depend upon large government spending they were ready to embrace Ronald Reagan's crusade to restrict the public sector.[5]

Still, maybe government purchases shrink unemployment and compress wage gaps through other channels, provided that tax rates on labor are not pushed up to finance these purchases. That is, perhaps the natural unemployment rate itself is reduced by large public expenditures. Quantitative international studies do not provide significant support for that thought.[6] The special character of some public expenditures may make a difference, though. Most labor economists regard Sweden's jobs program for the unemployed as effective in reducing total unemployment; their impression is that the program's intake of workers from the unemployment pool does not set in motion a process of rising wages that ultimately refills that pool to its previous level. If they are right, however, the reason may be that the jobs program is "workfare"—the workers' welfare benefits are cut off once jobs are found for them—which makes the prospect of unemployment considerably less attractive than does the lifetime welfare provided the unemployed in the rest of Europe.

Many black American leaders also believe that employment programs in the public sector would improve black wages and employment. It is not obviously wrong to see the federal and state governments as capable of raising employment in their communities. When a large federal employer moves to Harlem, *employment* increases in Harlem and decreases outside Harlem—if only because some employees follow the employer to Harlem because they want to keep their jobs and some Harlem residents take the federal jobs because they are more convenient than jobs farther away. But does *unemployment* in Harlem decrease? Do *wages* in Harlem increase?

Furthermore, there are some negative effects of a large government presence in the labor market of poverty areas. Pondering the problems in the south of Italy, the Italian economist Luigi Bonatti argues that for economic development to take place, most young people entering or approaching entry into the labor force must orient themselves toward a career in the infant sector of dynamic private firms—preparing any general skills that might be helpful and actively seeking entry-level jobs, both of which require effort. But the existence of a large-scale government sector, where jobs offer quite decent pay from the start and lifetime job security, encourages young people to take the easier route of waiting at home or doing pick-up jobs in the so-called secondary sector until a public job can be arranged. In weakening employees' attachment and performance in private-sector jobs, the prospect of landing one of these more comfortable (yet ultimately more limiting) public-sector positions tends to drive up the incentive wages required by private employers and to drive up the unemployment rate. Moreover, when a private firm grasps the difficulty and uncertainty of attracting an adequate flow of suitable new recruits, it is apt to trim its expansion plans accordingly; the region exerts a drag on the dynamism of the firms.[7] New research at the World Bank, led by Mary Shirley, also finds a great many ill effects in developing countries from the government's large role (through state-owned enterprises and state agencies) as an employer and producer.[8]

On this view, the appreciable expansion of the public sector that has developed since the 1960s in Europe, especially France and Italy, has helped raise or at any rate prop up low wage rates and contributed to the rise of unemployment. In the United States, though, where the public sector has contracted, the change has not been large enough to matter much.

Addressing Inequities

America has been quite faithful to a central part of its free-market liberalism: the ideal that markets should be open to all who would be buyers or sellers, so that all are free to bid. Our historic antitrust legislation and the recent deregulation movement are intended to prevent vested interests from excluding others as well as to lower prices to the consumer by encouraging competition. Two other ideals, careers open to talents and equality before the law, are in the same tradition. (Yet there are anomalies. Legislation protects the rights of unions to use strikes and other threats to drive up members' wages notwithstanding that the increased labor costs may cause some to be excluded and driven to other industries to face lower wages than they would otherwise have earned. The defense must be a claim that people have an equal chance to get into these unions—that they are open to all races and ethnic groups.)

Another policy principle in America is the notion of fairness that is shown when we give the underdog a leg up. This is most evident in education. Since the early nineteenth century the country has provided free education to a much larger proportion of the population than any other nation, first at the elementary and high school levels and later in higher education. And in contrast to Europe's differentiated *lycées, gymnasia,* and grammar schools, it has aimed to reduce the impact of class background on education by setting up common standards.[9] Intensified education for disadvantaged children was instituted in the 1960s with Operation Head Start.

The government's activity on behalf of these two principles surely helps a great many of the disadvantaged to pull themselves up. It has been especially helpful to those having the talent to get ahead. It has facilitated the escape of people from the lower rungs of the job ladder. Yet it has done little if anything to raise the wages of those who remain on the lowest rungs.

Recent decades provide an unusually good opportunity to estimate the empirical effects of education on wages and unemployment. Federal expenditure (adjusted for inflation) on education per student tripled between the late 1960s and the early 1990s, as Senator Daniel Patrick Moynihan has often noted. Yet if statistical studies are a guide, there has been no salutary effect of such expenditure on the wage gap or the unemployment gap. A huge rise in the supply of workers completing high school and of workers with some years of college has also occurred in recent decades. Yet statistical research does not suggest it has operated in the direction of raising the wages in the lower rungs from which those workers came, nor of lowering those wages (as argued by Gilles Saint-Paul, cited earlier).[10]

The most important program for less advantaged workers in recent years is the Earned Income Tax Credit. This program offers a subsidy, paid to the employee directly rather than the employer, for eligible low-wage workers. Proposed by Senator Russell Long in the 1970s and championed by President Reagan in the 1980s, when it was signed into law, it was originally conceived as a way to counter the burden of payroll taxes on the wage income—the earned income, in the lexicon of public finance—of low-income people. (The credit increases with an eligible worker's wage income at a flat rate until reaching a cap; at some larger wage income the tax credit then begins decreasing with wage income at a flat rate—like a tent with a flat top.) What developed, however, was a tax credit limited to parents of young children. So the rationale was not so much to do something to pull up the reward to work of low-wage persons as it was to improve the living conditions of children of working people earning low wages. (Recent changes in the program offer an extremely scaled down credit to workers without dependent children.)[11]

This program, now running at more than $30 billion annually, has surely operated to pull up the after-tax-and-credit wages available to low-wage workers in the aggregate; where it has done so it has also served to improve employee motivation (at given hourly labor costs for employers) and thus to stimulate more hiring and ultimately reduced unemployment. But the program has, leaving aside the very recent change, done nothing to help raise the reward to work and the employment of single persons—men and young women choosing between employment and child raising. In fact, it can be argued that they are harmed. According to any standard economic analysis, the tax credit program operates to *reduce* the wage of low-wage workers before the tax credit is taken into account—to reduce weekly paychecks unadjusted for prospective credits. (A loose analogy is this: if the government sends checks in the mail to qualified barbers, the market wage for cutting hair will drop, although those getting the checks will gain overall, which is why they will supply more to the industry and thus drive down the before-check wage.) For those workers not qualifying for the tax credit, therefore, the effect must be a *reduction* in their wage before and after taxes.

Reducing Insecurity

The last category of government activity includes the programs of social insurance aimed at reducing people's economic insecurity. The objective is to lessen the downside risk (the amount they stand to lose) in the event of unfavorable contingencies.

The social assistance programs of the welfare system, by providing cash and in-kind benefits to the destitute and the needy, pare the losses that people will bear if they (or their close relatives or friends) become destitute or face outsized needs. The hallmark of the welfare programs is their use of a means test (comparing means against needs) to determine eligibility.

The programs include Medicaid for the indigent (1.53 percent of the Gross Domestic Product in 1990), the food stamp and child nutrition programs (0.45 percent in 1990), Supplemental Security Income for the blind and the elderly and disabled not otherwise covered (0.31), lower-income housing assistance and public housing (0.31), Title 20 benefits for child care (0.09), and the states' general assistance programs (0.06). Unemployment insurance benefits (0.29 percent) are not means-tested in the normal way, but they are conditional on the absence of wage income, so this program fits well enough in the welfare category. Aid to Families with Dependent Children (0.38 percent) amounts to nearly one-tenth of the total of these programs.

In a quite different class are the programs under Old Age Survivors and Disability Insurance (some 10 percent of net national product)—known familiarly as social security. There is no means test to receive its retirement benefits; these programs prevent destitution rather than waiting for it to happen. And they are work-related—a reward for working the required number of years.

The expansion of the welfare system since 1960 has been quite expensive. Its spending went from 1½ percent of the gross domestic product in 1960 to about 2 percent in 1970 to almost 4 percent in 1990. This increase amounts to $140 billion per annum. (There are more people to serve now than three decades ago, but there are also more people to produce the GDP, so the increased population does not create a case for increasing welfare's share of the GDP.)

The rise of this large welfare system represents a departure in political economy, to use the older term for the study of economic policy. From the early nineteenth century, discussion of the good economy has customarily centered on the structure of rewards for work. The starting point is the gain from economic collaboration: when people work together in their country's economy each participant does better than by producing alone in the wild or in separate camps, and so it is important to the citizenry that this social surplus be distributed equitably among them—the only issue being what, exactly, is equitable. One conception of equity was the equalitarianism of the old socialist tradition in Britain and parts of the European continent. A twentieth-century conception endorses big rewards to those at the high end of the income distribution as long as their effects on entrepreneurship and so on serve to lift rewards at the low end. Elements of this view—rooting for the underdog without spite toward the top dogs—are part of American tradition. The rationale of the welfare system, though, does not rest on any notion of just rewards for contribution.

In the philosophy underpinning the welfare system the good economy is one with the widest possible cushion, or safety net—the fully cushioned economy. This "welfarism," to use a term of the economist-philosopher Amartya Sen, looks at people's resources (and any special needs) and seeks to send resources to where they are low (in relation to needs) in order to increase aggregate well-being. No attention is paid to who is doing what with whom—hence no attention to whether the recipients are participating in the economy in any productive way.[12] People whose income is low or nil are entitled to free medical care, drug rehabilitation, emergency shelter, aid for their young children, and so forth whether or not they are in the labor force.

These entitlements, many conservatives complain, are not conditional on any reciprocal responsibilities. Moreover, the budgetary obligations that these entitlements pose for workers fall outside the associative duties, in the current term, that workers (and contributors generally) have toward one another.[13] However, it is not with these moral issues that we are concerned here.

The welfare programs *could* have been made contingent upon the recipients' employment. Bismarck's famous social insurance innovations—health insurance and accident insurance for workers and old age and invalidity insurance—were all work-related, intended to sweeten the reward to work for those not able to find such insurance in the private market (or not disciplined enough buy it). But the pressures to universalize must have been hard to resist, especially when the costs of doing so seemed small. Today, only a minority of social insurance entitlements, such as unemployment insurance, are restricted to workers, and some work-related entitlements, such as social security benefits, are only weakly work-related.

This welfare system, I will now argue, adds to the volume of unemployment in the economy, especially that of low-wage workers, and widens the gap between the rewards of workers in the lower half and those in the middle. Expansion of the system expands these effects. There are at least three channels through which this welfare system has effects on employment and wages, particularly of the disadvantaged. These are social wealth, means-testing, and payroll-tax financing.

Social Wealth

The decoupling of work from benefit in the typical welfare program is a key to a whole class of neglected effects of welfare programs on wages and employment. If eligibility for benefits is not conditional on employment, past or present, it does not have to be earned through the contribution of one's work to the economy. Thus the system undercuts the original purpose of work, which is to make a living. If workers do not have to have a job in order to receive disability benefits if impaired, food stamps if their income is low, medical benefits if ill, and housing if homeless, the motive for working is badly weakened.

The proposition may be stated another way. The award of these entitlements immediately adds to what we may call people's social wealth. If this system were financed through taxation of their private tangible and financial wealth—levies on their marketable assets such as their homes, cars, boats, and securities—the income or services after tax on this private wealth would be reduced by just enough to pay for the flow of welfare payments; hence their private wealth would be down in the aggregate by exactly as much as their social wealth was up, leaving aggregate wealth unchanged. But the system is financed largely out of wages—through payroll taxes, income taxes, and sales taxes. Thus *human* wealth, which is the economic value of the natural abilities and the value of the investment in education, called human capital, is reduced.

This windfall of benefits, benefits that do not have to be earned, is very much like being born with a silver spoon in your mouth. Your human wealth is effectively devalued. The classical effect of this—the effect emerging from supply and demand—is simply a contraction of labor supply, resulting in a reduction in the labor force. An economist from Iceland and collaborator of mine, Gylfi Zoega, has noticed, perhaps from having grown up in a welfare state that goes further than ours, that the social wealth created by the welfare system is much more pervasive than this.[14]

A familiar effect is that unemployed workers are less motivated to take the first job that comes along. This may lead to long-term unemployment that hardens into unemployability. The effects on employed workers, introduced in Chapter 4, are at least as important. The increased social wealth affects their job attachment, making them less motivated to be good employees. A great many will succumb to the temptation to slack off more at work and to quit more readily. A consequence is increased labor costs, which force up the unemployment rate. Obviously it is the unemployment rate of low-wage workers that is most affected, generally speaking, since the welfare entitlements to be gained from not working are only worth considering by workers with poor or mediocre wage-earning opportunities. It is also possible that the deterioration in the performance of low-wage workers results in a *fall* of their wage, not the rise to which the classical supply-demand argument points.

The conclusion, then, is that the welfare system, in creating social wealth, has effects on workers' motives that both enlarge the volume of structural unemployment (the so-called natural rate) and shrink the labor force. And there is every reason to believe that it is among low-wage workers—not high-wage workers, who do not factor food stamps into their thinking—that the social net has the biggest impacts on morale, adding to joblessness and worsening productivity.

Is it true? Theory, like wishing, does not make a proposition so. But there is now some statistical evidence pointing to an effect of entitlement spending on unemployment rates.[15] There have also been studies of particular elements of the welfare system. The degree to which unemployment insurance benefits replace the wage income lost when a person becomes unemployed has also been found to be a statistically significant influence, though not awfully important in quantitative terms; it is, after all, just one tiny element in the amalgam of welfare programs.

Does all this mean that the welfare system makes the disadvantaged worse off? It is the famous thesis of Charles Murray that the welfare state has indeed caused the disadvantaged to lose ground.[16] His argument is that the availability of welfare assistance widens the number of young women choosing single parenting of children over the early jobholding of others their age, and that their prolonged use of this assistance, in diverting them from the experience of jobholding, causes them to lose self-confidence and employability. My thesis is quite different: that a pro-employment policy that draws upon and builds up the low-wage workers' capacity for self-help is better for everybody and, if instituted, would cause welfare to wither away.

Nevertheless, one can argue along the lines already laid out here that welfare does do more harm than good. In a world of just one worker, of course, the arrival of a sort of natural welfare—like manna from heaven—would induce this lone individual to work less and work less well, so his or her earned income would suffer; but total potential income (at given level of work and its intensity) would be up so the worker could not be worse off. In a society of many workers, though, the arrival of welfare may very well make them generally worse off. For when, in response to the resulting decline of job attachment and consequent rise in costs, employers cut back jobs in the community, the rise in the unemployment rate imposes burdens on every worker. Employed workers whose job attachment is undiminished by whatever welfare entitlements might be of help to them will find themselves at greater risk of losing their own jobs and may even find their wages reduced, as their employers practice statistical discrimination. Workers having a spell of unemployment can expect to need a longer time to find work again. Thus those workers receiving the largesse of the welfare system and responding with reduced job loyalty and performance generate a negative "externality" on the rest of the labor force. And if, in response to the long wait to get a job and the increased sense of powerlessness, a culture of drugs and crime grows up, there is obviously a further set of negative externalities.

Means-Testing

The second channel through which the welfare system damages disadvantaged workers is created by the means-testing. Welfare programs, though not work-related, are very much income-related. If only persons with incomes below a certain level are eligible for a welfare entitlement, and if becoming employed will increase a person's income enough to make him ineligible for the entitlement, then employment and the entitlement are mutually exclusive. The one must compete against the other. In this contest, work cannot be competitive with welfare unless its pay at least approaches the benefit provided by the entitlement. After all, when the rewards of both work and welfare are very small, even a small difference in favor of welfare may take precedence over other considerations, at least for some length of time.

In fact, as is widely known but perhaps still underestimated, a great many welfare recipients are receiving appreciably more from their entitlements than most of them could expect to earn in the marketplace. Recall the welfare outlay cited in Chapter 2, some $150 billion (plus $35 billion in somewhat similar outlays). If the recipients were one-tenth of the labor force, thus 13 million, the payment per recipient would be around $13,000—some receiving more, a majority receiving less. If all this welfare were cut off and these recipients had to rely on wages, it is doubtful that half—or even a quarter—of them would earn that much in wages in a typical year. This is all very aggregative. Until lately we have lacked precise estimates of the total benefit to any particular class of welfare beneficiary.

A recent estimate of the total welfare payments to single parents finds a much stronger balance in favor of welfare over work. Stephen Moore and Michael Tanner begin with the point that, although welfare advocates portray Aid to Families with Dependent Children payments to single mothers as woefully small, admittance into the AFDC program paves the way to eligibility for several other welfare programs.[17] On a reasonably full accounting, the welfare package comes to more than $12 an hour in five states, more than $10 an hour (which is around the median wage) in seventeen states, and more than $8 an hour in forty states. These pay rates are far above what all but a small proportion of the recipients could expect to earn in the economy—before tax or after tax.

True, single parents draw most heavily on the welfare system and the great majority of single parents are women. On the face of it, few men are eligible under the system, unemployment insurance excepted. (This is in sharp contrast to the system in Canada.) Yet the life of men in America's poor communities is nearly as much shaped by our welfare system as that of women. Since the male partner of a welfare mother would jeopardize her eligibility were they to marry and cohabit, owing to the means test, and since he cannot typically bring in enough wages with enough reliability to compete with welfare, he cannot contribute enough to play the stabilizing and organizing role of husband and father. Men, far from seeing their motives to work and earn and realize their potential left intact by the welfare system, are instead threatened with emasculation by it.

Somewhat similarly, the huge rise in social security retirement benefits has undercut the role that men (and women) in the labor force might play as earners of income with which to supplement the resources of their aged parents. In fact, retirement benefits, which have grown large relative to wages in the past two decades, have the perverse effect of adding indirectly to the nonwage support that working-age men might count on from their retired parents. These features of the American welfare system operate to reduce their availability for work and, when employed, their job attachment.

Payroll-Tax Financing

The third channel through which the welfare system damages disadvantaged workers is the method of financing social insurance. Several social insurance programs are financed by payroll taxation—social security for retirees, workman's compensation for accidents, and unemployment insurance, mainly. This taxation adds to the labor costs (specifically the nonwage labor costs) of production and thus, as noted in Chapter 6, reduces the after-tax wage that employers can afford to pay without having to cut back the number of their employees. Of course, this reduction of the after-tax wage is not tantamount to a reduction of the net total reward from employment; some employees may feel that the social insurance provided fully compensates them for the cut in the paycheck—that they are getting their money's worth.

If they do feel they are fully compensated for the pay cut, there is no further effect on unemployment, labor force participation, or anything else. But it seems quite unlikely that this will generally be the case, especially for low-wage workers. For employees earning a low or moderate wage, the payroll tax is quite large in relation to the wage. The tax comes to about 20 percent of take-home pay until the tax reaches a cap, or ceiling. These workers, and not only these, may feel that they are getting less than their money's worth. If so, there will be a further effect on unemployment and the labor force among the disadvantaged.

One reason payroll taxes are so high is that citizens do not want to be burdened by the destitution of persons who have been improvident or unlucky in accumulating wealth for their old age or for contingencies such as unemployment or an industrial accident. The taxpayers prefer not to pay each worker's insurance premium for him—their idea is to escape such burdens, not simply to redesign them—but instead to mandate that each worker pay his own insurance premium, whether or not he sees it as a worthwhile bargain. In the United States there is the complication that social security is a pay-as-you-go system, meaning that today's contributions pay immediately for the benefits of today's retirees. That feature of the system has added an even more powerful impetus toward exorbitant rates and benefits. Every generation or so a majority of the older members of the population can make themselves better off by legislating a further increase of benefit levels, seeing that the burden of the higher tax rate to finance them will be mostly shouldered by the younger minority. This game—a sort of Ponzi scheme—is now reaching its limit. But there may be no politically palatable way to engineer a rollback of the benefit and tax rate levels.

Another reason the payroll tax rate may far exceed what low-wage workers would be willing to pay for the benefits is that the better-paid workers want a comparatively lavish set of protections. Having relatively high income, they are better able to afford them. And since their benefits are not taxed (except unemployment benefits) while their wages are heavily taxed, they will trade off more than a dollar of wages to get a dollar of benefits—up to a point. Hence the better-paid will give their voting support to a much higher level of the flat payroll-tax rate than the level preferred by the low-paid.

A further reason disadvantaged workers might feel they are getting less than full value for their money is that they may assume that a range of their social insurance benefits could be duplicated, perhaps on a much reduced scale, through private charitable sources. And, being disadvantaged, they would not expect to be burdened with providing charity to others.

Yet another factor is that, as noted earlier, benefits were on a strongly rising trend until the mid-1970s, thanks to productivity growth and population growth in the economy. So workers could expect that their retirement benefit represented a good return on their "investment" of their payroll tax into the system. That is no longer so. Further, since interest rates are higher, the discounted value of the future pension benefits has dropped even more. For these reasons workers must have come to regard the worth of their benefits as vastly smaller in relation to their wages than was the case two or three decades ago.

This decline in the total reward to work operates to push up unemployment. In response to the payroll tax, employers cut wages enough to "pass along" the whole payroll tax to the workers, expecting thus to regain a normal profit. If disadvantaged workers then feel that, on the whole, the total reward to jobholding is diminished on balance despite the welfare entitlements, the effect will be to decrease their job attachment. The fall in the reward to work will elevate these employees' propensity to quit, to shirk, to be absent from work, to go on strike, and so forth, since the earnings they would lose if they quit or were fired are now reduced. As a consequence, employers' costs are increased. (Employers may partly restore wages in order to restore employee performance, partially or fully, but doing so will still leave costs higher than they were prior to the introduction of the payroll tax.) There results a contractionary effect on employment. The natural unemployment rate is pushed up.[18]

Yet, as noted in Chapter 6, in the long run, the affected workers will tend to cut back their rates of saving in response to the increased waiting times in the unemployment pool and the decrease in take-home pay. As a result, their private wealth will start to decline. The decline of wealth will increase their dependence on work and thus operate to improve their job attachment. The natural unemployment rate will thus tend to fall back. Much, though not all, of the increased unemployment resulting from the emergence of the mature welfare state will thus be transitory. But this mechanism applies less to the disadvantaged, many of whom were not saving to begin with.

To summarize: the welfare programs that are not work-related, such as Medicaid and food stamps, devalue work and thus reduce job attachment. Means-testing intensifies the impact. The work-related programs, such as social security and workman's compensation, are financed by payroll taxation. In both cases, labor costs are increased; employers pass the increase along to workers in the form of reduced wages, which in turn result in increased unemployment. The effect is proportionately stronger on workers at a given place in the wage distribution the lower their wage. So wage rates are reduced relatively more, and unemployment rates increased more, the lower the wage rate of the workers we consider. The wage gap is widened and likewise the gap in unemployment rates. These effects are unlikely to be negligible when these same welfare programs loom large enough to have visible effects on lifestyles and attitudes in entire communities in other realms—in illegitimacy rates, drug use, and juvenile crime.

Wage earning and jobholding are now dwarfed as a way of life by the welfare system. Welfare pays more than work for the mothers eligible for AFDC and the train of benefits that follow from it.

In the United States there is ample reason to believe that such a massive attack on the primacy of employment constitutes a threat to the viability of disadvantaged communities. The decline of morale and the increased joblessness are bound to undermine the work ethic, leading to increased criminality and drug use, which in turn further threaten young workers coming of age in these communities.

The Remedy

8

.

The Market-Based Solution

The problem has now been described. The pay of America's lowest lifetime earners has become so remote from the pay of the median earner as to make them a class apart, with radically diminished possibilities next to those in the mainstream. By buying more education they can expect to restore their relative wage, but there is a toll on that escape route, so it can only moderate the loss. The gulf in pay, by sapping their initiative and hindering their access to middle-class institutions, casts a pall over poor communities and leaves a legacy of disadvantage for the next generation.

Since mid-century the gap has only grown. The relative wage of unskilled men drifted down in the 1950s and 1960s, as machines replaced much strongback labor. Then their relative wage began a steep slide, joined a decade later by the relative wage of unskilled women—a slide that has only recently come to a halt. The crumbling of the old wage pattern reached to the working class, where many of their high-wage manufacturing jobs were lost. The main forces behind these shifts in wages, such as information technology, are unlikely to reverse themselves.

This devaluation of work imposes costs throughout society. When the less advantaged saw their wages rise far less than the rest, some, especially men, were led away from work into drugs and crime. When their productivity and thus their wages declined,

103

their private assets did not show reduced returns and their social wealth was not hit by cutbacks in benefits; that was largely because the productivity of others and national income did not decline (it rose). So their pay fell relative to the part of their support that is not conditional on their working. Hence their work made less of a difference to them. Most of the surge in joblessness among the less advantaged since the 1960s and the accompanying rise in several indicators of social breakdown—the steep rise in the rates of illegitimacy and violent juvenile crime in areas of concentrated poverty, the outbreaks of drug use, and the increased incarceration—is an outgrowth of this decline in the reward to work relative to other support. As the body politic rejected solidarity with disadvantaged workers, so they abandoned responsibility toward others and even toward themselves. The bill for their abdication is left for the rest of society to pay.

The working class too have reacted to the devaluation of their work—with the politics of rage. Observing that the government provides welfare benefits to support large numbers who do not work at all, they demand that the government not stand idly by as market forces cast them one by one out of their high-wage jobs into unfamiliar low-wage work. To garner votes from the working class the political parties have been eager to grant them various social protections, from the repudiation of free trade to increased rights against employers. The public is asked to believe that these policy moves are cheap for the rest of society, maybe even a net benefit. In fact, though, the price of these policies to mollify the working class is far more costly (for a given level of resulting benefit) than a policy going to the root of the problem, the decline in the market value of work.

The solution to this problem is to raise the wage of lesser-paid work that business can afford to pay relative to the income and services received by the less well paid independently of their work. Just as the downhill slide of wages relative to wealth among the less advantaged has fueled increases in their idleness, criminality, and illegitimacy, having negative external effects on the rest of society, so reversing that slide through a program to pull up wages relative to wealth among the disadvantaged would benefit the rest of society by reducing those negative external effects.

It might seem that, to implement that solution, lowering or taking away the safety net must be the instrument of choice. To raise the ratio of pay to social wealth among the disadvantaged, just decrease the denominator: reduce entitlements in order to decrease their social wealth relative to the wage business can afford to pay them. Then watch them scurry for jobs. But rolling back welfare benefits and eligibility requirements to 1965 levels, say, would not go very far toward solving the problem—valuable though it might be in conjunction with the genuine solution. It would bring only a modest improvement in unemployment rates and little if any recovery in relative wage rates—just as the *expansion* of the welfare system after 1965 can plausibly account for only a modest increase in unemployment and little if any of the decline in relative wages among low-wage workers. After all, the welfare system is just one part of the social support system; and rolling it back to 1965 levels would not mean the end of these programs.

Never having had a safety net when the productivity of disadvantaged labor fell over the past generation would have averted a magnification of the effect on unemployment. But not even the most hawkish proponents of a return to the free market envisage removal of the safety net. Eliminating the welfare system would carry a large risk. We cannot have any reliable idea of how society would fare without food stamps, Medicaid, and the rest. (In the 1920s the country was more rural and established charities were more up to the task of mitigating destitution than they could be now.) We must assume at least a minimal welfare system, despite its side effects on unemployment, wages, self-reliance, and self-respect.

A Low-Wage Employment Subsidy

The natural solution is an employment subsidy.[1] The essence of such a program is that the government makes periodic contributions to reward employment of workers in eligible low-wage jobs at qualified enterprises. In the scheme I favor, the periodic government disbursement goes to each qualified *enterprise* for every low-wage worker in its employ. All employees having the same wage are to bring in the same subsidy to the employer. The government contributes the same additional subsidy with every additional employee costing the employer a given hourly amount. (Payroll taxes are similarly comprehensive and blind to everything but pay.)

Consider, for example, those employees whose hourly *wage cost* to their employer ends up at $4 after allowance for the employment subsidy. This wage cost equals the "wage"—more accurately, the wage of the employees gross of their payroll tax contributions—*less* the subsidy contributed by the government.[2] The $4 contribution that firms are making is the measure of the private productivity of these employees' work, as estimated by their employer. The government's hourly contribution to jobs having so low a market value for employers would desirably be a substantial amount, say $3. Then these workers' *hourly wage* would be $7, gross of their part of the payroll tax.

The subsidy is thus like a matching grant rewarding the firm for as many workers as it employs, particularly workers whose private productivity is low (as evidenced by the low hourly labor cost that firms are willing to incur for their services). It is the low-productivity workers whose possibility of self-support and cohesion with the mainstream of society is impaired and whose job attachment and social responsibility are undermined when they are paid a wage to match their low productivity, so it is these workers especially to whom the subsidies are to be targeted.

The rationale for employment subsidies can now be stated: the wage that private employers can afford to pay an employee is only the worker's *private* productivity—the productivity within the business—in the absence of employment subsidies or similar measures.[3] But society has an interest in seeing work and other contributions rewarded according to their *social* productivity. And the social productivity of work generally exceeds its private productivity, since there are external benefits for the rest of the citizenry from one's ability to support oneself and to exercise responsibility as a citizen, community member, parent, and spouse.

What is needed, then, is an employment subsidy from the government to supplement the worker's contribution to the enterprise by the amount of this *extra* productivity—the *external* productivity of the worker's employment, which makes little difference for the bottom line of the enterprise employing the worker (and a similarly small difference to every individual in the economy) but a significant aggregate difference to all members of society taken together. This subsidy device, calibrated to the correct size, can present employers with approximately the right incentives to employ low-wage workers and, in so doing, drive up their wage.

Before considering the wage and employment effects of the subsidies, it may avoid misunderstandings to anticipate some questions. Is all employment to be eligible? No. The objective of the subsidy is to restore the orientation toward employment of those who are able-bodied and mentally competent and to make such employment the basis for self-support and self-esteem. Hence those whose productivity level in enterprises would be negative or merely zero (as measured by the hourly wage cost their employers are willing to bear) are not to be eligible for the subsidy. And undoubtedly many would say that, even among workers whose productivity is positive, there is a productivity level so low that workers below it would not be capable of the self-development and strengthened responsibility that the subsidy program aims to achieve. So the subsidy should be conceived as applying only to workers whom their employer sees as worth bearing a significant cost to employ. Hence the government's contribution kicks in where the employer's hourly contribution reaches some floor, or minimum. (I take the floor hourly wage cost to be somewhat below the statutory minimum wage in current law; even so, the corresponding subsidy will bring about an hourly wage well above the statutory minimum.)

Another question concerns the scope for abuses of the scheme. The subsidies might best take the form of tax credits against the firm's payroll tax, corporate income tax, and any other tax liabilities (federal, state, or local). In that way the plan will combat the rise of "subsidy mills" that enlist people not to produce but to defraud the government by inventing labor costs with which to claim cash subsidies that would be shared between the "employees" and the "employer." There will still be risks of fraudulent featherbedding. But in the information age, it is inexpensive to run a computer check for a person's holding of multiple payroll-tax-eligible and therefore subsidy-eligible jobs.

It would be best on the whole to restrict the subsidies to full-time jobs of low-wage employees—say, 35 hours a week or more. Since the aim is to draw the unemployed and those out of the labor force or only fitfully in it into a life of full-time jobholding and career-building, so that they become self-supporting and have a better chance of realizing their abilities, it appears desirable to exclude part-time jobs from the subsidies. Also, firms need then only declare that a job was full-time (subject to penalties for false declaration) and report the qualifying weekly or monthly wage to receive the subsidy; hours worked each week will not have to be tabulated.

Another desirable feature of the subsidies is that they are restricted to profit-seeking enterprises, which means as a practical matter firms in the private sector. Of course state enterprises also pay some attention to their bottom line, since the government has a limit to the state-enterprise deficits it can underwrite. But state enterprises are apt to have high-employment and high-wage programs of their own, and not always for the benefit of the disadvantaged. The purpose of the wage subsidy is not to fortify the spoils system of job patronage but rather to encourage gainful employment by the less productive members of the labor force. In confining the employment subsidies to the private sector the government would be encouraging employment of low-productivity workers without becoming directly involved in the business of estimating the productivity of each prospective employee. The wage cost that a private employer is willing to bear is a signal to the government of the employee's productivity at that firm in the judgment of the firm.

The Case of a "Flat" Employment Subsidy

Employment subsidy schemes tend, generally speaking, to drive both the wages and the unemployment rates of low-wage workers in the direction we want. The main channels stand out clearly in the example of a flat hourly subsidy—such as $3—for *all* jobs, not just low-wage jobs, meeting the restrictions noted above.

After the introduction of the flat subsidy, the revenue (net of interest and depreciation on the associated investment) generated by employees consists of their net productivity *plus the subsidy.* This supplemented revenue gives the gross wage (gross of their payroll-tax deduction) that the employer can afford to pay such workers while maintaining their number intact through hiring and training to offset attrition—the affordable wage for a normal profit. Clearly, every dollar of this supplement adds a dollar to the affordable gross hourly wage, increasing it in our example by $3.

Let us now focus on the long run and assume that, in an economy as open as the American economy, small or moderate structural shifts have little permanent effect on global interest rates. In that case, the subsidy has no impact on net productivity through interest rates and interest cost. Hence the addition to revenue just mentioned is the sole impact of the subsidy on the affordable wage—the whole effect before any adjustment of employment occurs.

In contrast, the subsidy has no impact at all on the wage required by incentive considerations—no effect before adjustment of employment. This is true in the long run, after workers have adjusted their wealth to their wage, which is what matters for the end-effects on employment and wages. (On impact, before wages and employment have responded, the subsidies add to profits, which adds to workers' nonwage incomes, thus lessening their job attachment and forcing up the required incentive wage; but in the long run workers will decumulate or accumulate wealth as needed to bring their wealth back in line with their wage, so this short-run impact has no final significance.)

What, in view of these impacts, are the consequences of the subsidy for wages and unemployment? The ruling principle determining where things go is that the market wage, which we may think of as given by the required incentive wage, must be equal to the affordable wage; and employment must adjust up or down to achieve this reconciliation. If the affordable wage remained in excess of the incentive wage, firms would be left receiving a profit exceeding the normal return they need to make on their investment. Market competition eliminates opportunities for "free money" in the same way nature abhors a vacuum. The firms cannot swallow the subsidy for their owners, since their competition for workers, who are at first generating more revenue than before, ensures that their wages rise until the abnormal profit is eliminated. (Empirical economics abounds with case studies of how payroll taxes, for example, end up being passed along to the workers involved.)[4]

The adjustment process brings a decrease in unemployment. In boosting the wage that firms can afford to pay above the wage that cost considerations require them to pay, the subsidy lifts the profit received on each initial employee. That stimulates firms to hire more employees, including low-wage workers—pulling their employment up, their unemployment down. This tightening of the labor market in turn drives up the incentive wage firms are impelled to pay—the required wage—and thus tends to close the gap with the affordable wage. Thus the gross wage will rise until the unemployment rate among workers of any given productivity has fallen to the point where the required (and actual) wage is once again equal to the affordable wage.

What of the net wage—after tax? Ultimately there will *not be* any extra taxes needed if the subsidy program is self-financing, as contended in the next chapter. A detailed look at the effects of tax financing in the interim is best deferred, yet the main conclusion is clear: On the one hand, the fixed worker-subsidy, whatever the method of financing, raises the annual gross wages of all workers by the same absolute amount. On the other hand, a flat tax rate on payrolls or incomes tends to lower all after-tax wage rates in equal proportion (one complication aside). Hence the *lower* net wage rates rise on balance while the higher net wage rates fall on balance.

Would a flat subsidy—putting aside the question of whether there are better designs—be a good policy instrument? Some distinguished economists have thought so. For years such a scheme has been carefully studied and repeatedly advocated by the British labor economists Richard Jackman and Richard Layard. Although they assume, taking the worst case, that every shilling of outlay would have to be financed by a flat-rate tax on payrolls, they see great merit in its contraction of unemployment and its lift to pay rates of low-wage workers.[5]

Note that the flat employment subsidy is fundamentally different from an invention of another era—the so-called Negative Income Tax proposed by Milton Friedman in the early 1960s. That was a flat lump-sum entitlement payable to every adult and child in the country, regardless of current work status or work history. This became the "demogrant" of $1,000 per capita (about $3,000 in today's dollars) that George McGovern envisaged in the 1972 presidential campaign. Those of us who favored the plan at that time saw it as an improvement over the cumbersome welfare system—the melange of programs offering free food and shelter and medical care would be replaced by an annual cash grant to every household to be spent as it chose. It would be tidier, fairer, and, because it would not be means-tested, it would not penalize earning.

There was little appreciation of what a defect it was that such a substantial universal payment was not to be conditional on working.[6] On that logic, it would be quite all right, resources permitting, to award people reaching the age of majority lifetime supplies of everything they might want—as long as the scale of the gift did not discriminate against those who chose to work. All too many young people would lack the vision and the will to resist yet another year of avoiding life's challenges and risks.

In contrast, a fixed worker-subsidy *would* be conditional on employment. By pulling up wage rates it would serve to draw people out of unemployment, nonemployment, welfare, drugs, and crime into jobs; the Negative Income Tax would merely temper the tendency of welfare to keep people away from jobs and would do nothing to restore jobholding as the means of self-support and the vehicle for personal growth and the sense of belonging and being needed.

The drawback of the *flat* subsidy is that it expends the same subsidy on high-wage jobs, where the social benefit would be negligible, as on low-wage jobs. If the hourly subsidy were really flat at $3, in a normal workyear of some 2000 hours the subsidy would come to $6,000 per year. If that annual fixed subsidy were provided for the employment of all the 70 million full-time workers in the private sector, no matter how high their wage or salary, the annual expense for the government budget would amount to $420 billion. This outlay would be self-financing to some extent: with the resulting rise of national employment and output, there would be a significant increase in various fiscal revenues and a wide range of savings in various government programs. It is safe to say, though, that there would result a net increase in the all-government budgetary deficit of about $200 billion, perhaps more, which would require a significant rise in one or more tax rates. If the deficit were to be covered by a flat tax rate on full-time private payrolls, without any cap, a tax rate of about 10 percent would be required. Those employees whose total labor cost to their employer per annum is at the mean level, around $60,000, would break even (minor complexities aside). Whether or not such an additional tax rate would be a deterrent to enactment of the plan in that simple version, a more cost-effective design would be preferable.

Graduating the Wage Subsidy

The design we want is a graduated subsidy with the basic property that the subsidy declines as the hourly wage increases. It is also important that the subsidy decline slowly. Finally, it is desirable that the subsidy should decrease smoothly, rather than coming down to zero with a hard landing. In recent research the economist Hian Teck Hoon and I have explored the effects of such a graduated subsidy and studied its appropriate design.[7]

An illustration will serve to convey the essential structure. In the illustrative scheme, all qualifying jobs that have a net hourly labor cost to the employer of $4 (net of subsidy) are eligible for an hourly subsidy of $3, just as before. The corresponding hourly cost gross of subsidy, $7, is these employees' hourly compensation—their hourly wage including the employee-paid payroll tax. Jobs having a net hourly labor cost of $5 receive a smaller subsidy. But the decline of the subsidy is gentle enough that the hourly wage in these jobs is greater than $7. Precisely how the subsidy decreases with hourly cost is tabulated as follows:[8]

Wage cost per hour	Subsidy per hour	Gross wage per hour
$4.00	$3.00	$7.00
$5.00	$2.29	$7.29
$6.00	$1.65	$7.65
$7.00	$1.12	$8.12
$8.00	$0.71	$8.71
$9.00	$0.43	$9.43
$10.00	$0.24	$10.24
$11.00	$0.13	$11.13
$12.00	$0.06	$12.06

Under this schedule the wage of workers with the lowest productivity will be pulled up half the distance to the $10 mark, which is very roughly the median wage, while wage rates closer to that mark are pulled up by a smaller fraction of the gap. (In this range, then, wage differentials are cut in half or somewhat less, but not obliterated.)

Obviously the graduation in the above schedule has the basic property desired. It cuts down on outlays to employees whose wage rates are sufficient to place them a relatively safe distance from the hazards of welfare, unemployment, acute alcoholism, and crime. If there is more joy in heaven at the conversion of a sinner, then it makes sense to target the government's money where resulting conversions are a good bet.

The schedule also has the property that the subsidy does not decline too rapidly as we move to higher and higher hourly labor cost (or wage). If a firm could slash its labor expense at no cost to its moderately low-wage employees, because the subsidy payment would increase by just enough to offset the cutback by the firm in its own share of the paycheck, all low-wage workers would find their hourly wage set at $7 so all would warrant the maximum $3 hourly subsidy. The cost to the government would be considerably more than necessary and the wage gain to medium-low earners less than it could have been, given the total subsidy outlay. The illustrative schedule, in making the subsidy decline by less than a dollar with each dollar of hourly cost borne by the employer, does not invite that costly outcome. (A firm that chose to cut its hourly labor cost by $2, say, to reduce from $6 to $4 its cost of employing workers whose productivity is $6, would gain only a fraction of the $2 through the resulting increase in the subsidy, namely, an increase of only $1.35, from $1.65 to $3. So the firm would fall well short of the subsidy needed to pay these workers their going wage in the market.)

It has to be acknowledged that, despite the protections built into the schedule, employers will be tempted to defraud the government of additional subsidy income by reporting a reduced cash wage while not reporting that it is compensating the workers for the reduced paycheck through under-the-table benefits, most likely of a nonpecuniary nature—a parking place or whatever the employee will value highly. If providing these benefits will cost the employer less than his return—the cut in his cash payments to employees plus the gain in his subsidy—the deception will be profitable. Clearly, there must be penalties for such fraud, and firms must be monitored for the nonpecuniary benefits they extend to employees (just as they are already monitored by income-tax authorities). But keeping the rewards from such fraud at a low level by keeping the rate of tapering low would help to discourage fraud.

Another possible fraud to which the employment subsidies will be subject is a false claim by enterprises to have workers in their employ who are not working there. The employer could share the illegal gains with the phantom employees in order to buy their complicity. As a safeguard it will be necessary to limit a firm's subsidies to a credit against its payroll and profits taxes, and possibly to restrict eligibility to good-sized firms in which such flagrant fraud might become known to non-owners. Of course, the usual stiff penalties for tax evasion would be applied.

Finally, the illustrative plan displays the further property that the subsidy tapers off in a smooth fashion. If the subsidy hit zero sharply rather than smoothly, employers would see it as profitable, at least initially, to cut the pay of employees just outside the subsidy range in order to obtain a gain in subsidy that would be appreciable since these workers' jobs would not earn any subsidy at their initial pay. These workers would then find their pay reduced. (That might not be the final result, but the near-term future matters in politics.) The illustrative plan guards against that result, however. It does so by providing at moderate wage levels enough of a subsidy to ensure an increase of the wage rather than a decrease, as Hian Teck Hoon has shown.

What will be the effects of the graduated subsidy on wage rates and unemployment? They will be broadly similar to the effects of the flat subsidy. The wage rates in the relatively low-wage jobs will all be bid up and the unemployment of these workers pulled down. There is just one new wrinkle that ought to be noted. When the graduated subsidy is introduced, the employer who was formerly balancing the savings from lowering the wage in a job against the output costs of the reduced job performance that results will come to see that a small wage reduction will now bring in a larger subsidy. So the wage rates required by incentive considerations will be shifted down somewhat as a consequence of the graduation of the subsidy.

But this does not mean that the rise of wages in the lower reaches of the distribution is put in serious doubt. The wage rate must finally rise by the amount of the rise in the affordable wage, and the latter may very well have increased by the whole amount of the subsidy despite the decrease in unemployment (to which it may be relatively insensitive). In that case the end result, therefore, would be an extra boost to the *employment* of these workers but *not* an appreciably smaller increase of the wage than would have occurred without the graduation.

What will the budgetary cost of this graduated subsidy schedule be? A global look at the cost net of the various savings to the government and the taxpayer may be left for the next chapter. The *gross* budgetary cost is easily calculated if, to have a rough idea, we take as given the number of persons in each wage bracket—as if the program did not affect the level of employment of low-productivity workers. On that calculation, the cost would have been about $98 billion in 1990 (see the table at the back of this book). That expense would have been about $1\frac{3}{4}$ percent of the gross domestic product that year. If there were *no* budgetary savings and revenue benefits whatsoever, a flat-rate tax on full-time private payrolls of a little more than $2\frac{1}{2}$ percent would be approximately sufficient to finance the subsidy program.

To convert this estimate to 1997 terms one needs to adjust it for the small rise of money wage rates since 1990 and the growth of employment among low-wage earners. A rough calculation puts the 1997 cost at $110 billion. In addition, we should recognize that the resulting expansion of employment might add another $15 billion. The grand total is then $125 billion.

Methods of Interim Financing

Interim financing until the self-financing effects are at full force is a big subject for discussion. However, three possibilities stand out. One is a proportional, or flat-rate, tax on the payrolls of the same sector receiving the wage subsidies—the private sector, particularly its full-time employment. Another possibility not greatly different is a surtax on the personal income tax or simply an increase in income tax rates. The third possibility is an expenditure tax, or value-added tax. The last option has the drawback that it would entail introducing tax-collecting machinery that does not already exist. So, very probably, we are left with the first two possibilities. Perhaps it will suffice to examine the case of payroll-tax financing, especially since its effects would not differ greatly from those of income-tax financing.

Suppose, then, that the levy is a flat-rate tax on private full-time payrolls, so that the added payroll tax is proportional to the wage rate. If the subsidy were likewise a *proportional* wage subsidy, the two transactions would be a wash, the left hand undoing the right. But since the proposed wage subsidy does not rise proportionally to the wage—it actually decreases with the wage rate—the net result of the two opposing tendencies must ultimately be an increase in paychecks at the low end and a decrease in paychecks at the high end. In thinking about the effects on low-wage workers, at any rate, the flat tax rate on payrolls necessitated by the wage subsidies is so small (2½ percent until the revenue gains and savings flow in, it was estimated above) that we can neglect it.[10]

Cumulative forces set in motion by the new program will have some gradual effects. Seeing their wage rate increased, low-wage workers will respond by stepping up their saving, so their wealth will rise. The initial increase of the wage relative to wealth will tend to erode, causing their performance as employees to erode with it. This will steadily push up the incentive wage that employers need to pay or dampen employees' productivity—or both. With their labor costs being pushed up, the firms will allow their employment of these workers to begin to recede—but not all the way back to where it started. It is only at a decreased unemployment rate that the wage required for best incentives comes up to the increased level of the affordable wage that the subsidy has engineered.

What is the effect of this wage-subsidy, payroll-tax system on employment at the high end? At the high end, only the flat payroll-tax rate matters. Firms that used to pay their top talent $200 an hour will now calculate their worth to be about $195. The affordable wage is reduced. But the wage required by cost considerations—the best incentive wage—also drops. (The required wage drops because the payroll levy imposes an additional tax penalty on a firm's raising or restoring its employees' performance through a pay increase.) In the long run, when workers have adjusted their wealth to their lower wage, it will be found to have fallen exactly as much as the affordable wage has. The result is that employment of the high-wage workers will be found to be at the level it was originally. And the wage to the workers will have fallen by just enough to absorb the cost of the payroll tax.

Hiring Subsidies

There is a variant on the idea of employment subsidies, also known as wage subsidies. Why not simply give a subsidy for each *new hire?* Common sense would seem to commend it. That way, the government would not have to lay out subsidies for workers already employed. So the same steady level of total outlays would at first exert a powerful force pulling up employment and thus wage rates. But, of one hundred new jobs created, it would not be surprising if eight of the new employees quit each year and another two died or were let go each year, as in existing jobs. So the system of hiring subsidies would also entail an ongoing stream of outlays in the nature of depreciation. In addition the government would have to pay interest on the initial outlay that creates the new jobs. Nevertheless, the arithmetic here does make it appear that hiring subsidies are the better bargain.

There are two drawbacks to this variant, however. One catch is that firms would be tempted to abuse the system of hiring subsidies by trading their employees in order to generate additional subsidy revenues. Even a single corporation could create new business entities for the purpose of creating additional hiring subsidies. Setting up rules against such behavior and enforcing those rules might be a difficult task for the government.

The other difficulty arises from the fact that the hiring subsidies would effectively take the cost out of labor turnover for firms, since the cost of training a replacement would be covered, possibly more than covered, by the hiring subsidy. That would have the effect of reducing the unemployment rate, as firms no longer would have to vie with one another (at least not so intensively) to be the best-paying firm. This effect would be all to the good, of course. We want to see unemployment and thus the waiting times between jobs sharply reduced. But, with employees detached from the subsidy after their hiring, the employer and the employee alike would have less reason to invest in their relationship. This means that the firms would reduce the wage relative to employees' productivity. And productivity might erode through employees' reduced attachment to their jobs.

In any case, we do not need to resolve here the technical question of whether it is better to "front-load" the subsidy at the moment of hiring rather than to stretch it over the employee's duration in the job.

Two worries need to be addressed as part of this description of the graduated wage subsidy. (Chapter 11 will be devoted to a broader set of objections that have been raised against employment subsidies.) A great many listeners to the idea of a wage subsidy to pull up wages and employment of the working poor identify what they see as a danger in the plan. Won't employers seize upon the subsidy for the employment of low-wage workers to substitute them for higher-wage workers who would otherwise have been hired? The contention is that the latter workers will have to take a wage cut to be competitive in the labor market.

Perhaps this objection stems from thinking of a firm having a stock of customers today and no way to sell more to them. Then any additional hiring of the less productive workers must come at the expense of the more productive. But in the economy as a whole there is no such limitation on the output that can be sold—not in the space of a quarter-year or so, at least. The only real question is the extent to which the *productivity* of the more productive workers in the economy will be brought down by the employment of more workers from the ranks of the less productive. But, in general, the arrival of fresh supplies of any factor of production is expected to raise the productivity of the other factors, not lower it.

Recent studies of immigration of unskilled labor are relevant here. It is beginning to be reasonably well established that the influx of immigrants has caused only a modest reduction in the productivity of other workers—while, on the other side of the coin, it has pulled up the returns to land and capital (the latter temporarily, presumably). If this is the result after decades of appreciable immigration, it is hard to see how even a good-size reduction of unemployment among low-wage resident workers—and a one-time occurrence—would have appreciably adverse effects on the productivity of other workers. The wage subsidy would directly raise the wages of all workers below the median level. And workers whose productivity puts them above the median might very well be in occupations where their productivity would be raised by the additional supporting input of low-wage workers.

Another potential fear is that the welcome rise of wage rates in the lower half of the distribution produced by the graduated wage subsidy system will create pressure to raise the benefit levels of welfare programs in the same proportion. This is a dismal scenario, for if that were to happen it would reduce, if not altogether obliterate, the employment gain brought about by the wage subsidies. The incentive wages that employers required to keep down costs are not pushed up by the subsidies because the subsidies do nothing to raise workers' social wealth in the form of welfare entitlements (or their private wealth in the form of assets). If our welfare state were to take the wage increases as a signal to boost welfare benefits, the wage rates required for cost reasons would be pushed upward, tending to dampen if not offset the gains in employment.

Fortunately, experience suggests that welfare benefits are not tightly tied to wage rates at the low end. When wages for the least productive were dropping precipitously from the mid-1970s through the first half of the 1990s, there was no clear and general reduction of welfare benefit levels of a proportional nature. Some benefit levels were trimmed, but expenditures in some other programs increased. There is hope, therefore, especially if the need for caution is kept firmly in mind, that welfare outlays can be contained.

9

·

The Case for the
Market-Based Solution

Curiously for a country founded on broad opportunity and on the work ethic, America has no clear and explicit social policy toward the rewards to work—no policy aimed at ensuring that wages and available jobs do not fall so low for any group as to threaten that group's inclusion in the mainstream economy and its cohesion in our society.[1] The country has an express policy of mitigating destitution, now implemented by the welfare system. Unfortunately this system undermines the willingness and in some cases the ability of workers to support themselves in legitimate jobs and to exemplify self-reliance and responsibility in their families and communities. America also has an express policy of entitlements to social insurance. This insurance too is not a clear gain to workers, since workers have to bear an offsetting reduction of wages after payroll tax and possibly an attendant job loss until they have reduced (if they can) their private wealth to accord with their reduced wages and increased social wealth.

Behind the acceptance of the structure of wage rates is the public's inclination to trust in the rightness of the free market. Let consumers pay the free-market price of each good—the market price without the penalty of an excise tax or the benefit of a subsidy. The prices of clothes and cars and other goods ought to reflect the cost to society of producing them, and, according to laissez-faire doctrine, the prices of the *free* market do approximate those social costs, with few exceptions. Taxing or subsidizing a good, in raising or lowering its market price, would send the wrong signal, causing too little or too much to be purchased and produced—a distortion of the market. By the same token, let people earn the free-market wage for their services. (The public's main reservation appears to be that sellers should all be like hotels and cinemas, sticking to preannounced prices for their customers despite occasional excess demand, never like farm and oil producers, who seek the price that clears the market. Similarly, employers should stick to fixed wages despite occasional excess supply, laying off employees as required, except when solvency hangs in the balance.)

There is some irony here in that the late classical political economists who developed the argument for competitive markets, such as Marshall and Pigou, did not generally envisage that they were helping to establish laissez-faire. They bent over backward to produce examples in which the free-market price diverged from the *right* price. If the social cost exceeded (or fell short) of the private cost borne by producers, an excise tax (or subsidy) would be required to raise (or lower) the price to the level reflecting its social cost. Today we see the same dissonance between popular thinking and economic theory in the controversy over the gasoline tax.

It may be that there ought to be a presumption in favor of laissez-faire. The neoclassicals underestimated the danger that efficiency would suffer rather than gain if the price of every good was politicized by legislators second-guessing the free market. But there is little analogy between the price of individual goods and the terms of people's livelihood. And the public does countenance taxes on tobacco and gasoline, subsidies to farming and science.

The argument for low-wage employment subsidies to the private sector rests on the view that judicious subsidies are acceptable and even important in exceptional cases—as long as the system of free enterprise is kept firmly in place. Indeed, if low-wage workers become better rewarded, a more adventurous and less bridled capitalism might well be justified.

Wage rates, unemployment, and employment, the argument begins, have a special significance that does not attach to typical prices and outputs. When a large mass of workers can find work only at low wages, and especially when they are concentrated in poverty areas, these conditions have massive third-party effects of an adverse nature—negative external effects, or externalities. The presence of these effects provides a case for government intervention in the market for these workers through subsidies to moderate these negative effects.

Without an employment subsidy, the argument goes, competition in the marketplace drives up the weekly pay of workers only until it reaches the level of their weekly productivity (net of all payroll taxes) in the enterprise where they work. This productivity and the job satisfaction that the workers derive constitute the *private* benefit of these workers' employment. However, this productivity is only what they contribute within the walls of the enterprise. The philosophy behind the employment subsidy system is that the private benefit of employment does not fully capture—and hence the paycheck of the less productive workers does not fully reflect—the whole of the *social* benefit from these people's becoming employed workers. That social benefit is the private benefit going to their employer plus the external benefit to the rest of society from their position as participants in the business life of their community and the country, earning their own keep and supporting their children and setting an example for others growing up in their neighborhood.

The proposed low-wage employment subsidies will serve to narrow or close this divergence between private benefit and social benefit. The subsidies, in subtracting from the hourly labor cost of employing low-wage workers, will stimulate economy-wide hiring of such workers, driving down their unemployment rates and thus driving up their required pay and hence driving back up their hourly labor cost. When the expansion has reached the point where their hourly labor cost is again *equal* to their (net of tax) productivity, their hourly pay will be *higher* than their net productivity in the enterprise by the amount of the subsidy. The subsidy will have engineered a new *social wage* for low-productivity employees that reflects their job's productivity external to the enterprise employing them as well as its productivity internal to the enterprise. (The subsidy creates a beneficial wedge between paycheck and labor cost that counters and, for the more poorly paid, outweighs the bad wedge created by payroll taxes.)

The increase in the wage to low-wage workers is the remedy by which the negative external effects they were having on the rest of society can be curbed. Perhaps the curbing of criminal activity could be achieved instead by further increases in policing and sentences, but the major results in reduced unemployment and increased labor force participation, in reduced illegitimacy and reduced drug abuse, might be impossible to achieve by other means. These reductions in negative external effects—these external benefits from the added employment and increased self-support—accrue to the rest of society. The rest of society, as taxpayers, can afford to bear the budgetary cost of the subsidy program in exchange for external benefits, as long as the benefits cover the costs, without being worse off. Doing so is a sort of poetic justice. They may choose to do more.[2] However, if they do less there is no one else who will pick up the tab. There is no way in which the low-wage workers themselves can pay the cost of improving their rewards without largely undoing the improvement.

The ideal size of the subsidy to workers of a given private productivity would match the size of their external productivity— the excess of the social benefit over the private benefit from their employment. In that way the subsidy would provide the impetus for precisely the right increase in their pay. The total external benefit of an ideal subsidy is necessarily enough (or more than enough) to cover its cost to taxpayers since the subsidy is calibrated with these costs taken into account. The subsidies in the illustrative system presented in the previous chapter were not assumed to be of ideal size. That plan does not pretend to be the best articulation of the basic idea, only a plan that serves the purpose—to make deep inroads into unemployment and to achieve a major boost of pay rates among the less productive.

It is necessary, then, to evaluate whether the external benefit from the proposed plan is roughly commensurate with the subsidy outlay—particularly for the upper half of earners who may have to foot any extra taxes to pay for it.[3] (The subsidy also has a private benefit: the total receipts of the employment subsidies, most of which are passed on to low-wage workers. But this benefit is *their* benefit, not the benefit of those who will be asked to pick up the private cost.) To make the case for the wage subsidies we want to argue that the subsidy system would have external benefits *to those taxpayers footing the bill* that would be sufficient to repay their cost. In fact, I will argue that most of these external benefits would generate automatic budgetary savings and revenue gains that would alone pay the cost of the program. So tax rates would not have to be raised.

External Benefits of the Subsidies

There are four areas in which employment subsidies would confer external benefits—the same areas in which the dual phenomenon of relatively low wages and high unemployment has negative external effects. These areas of externality are the grounds for introducing the low-wage employment subsidy system—the political economy of the subsidy program.

Developmental Effects within Family and Community

As noted in Chapter 4, the rise of joblessness among less productive workers in recent decades has meant a decline in the number of parents who can serve as role models exemplifying self-reliance and strong job attachment. And the decline in the number of men able to be a substantial breadwinner has meant a rise in the number of families without any fathers at all. If these numbers are large enough, not only do the children in deprived families suffer but traditional norms within entire communities are subverted by new standards that take not working as the norm. (As noted in Chapter 7, the welfare system exacerbates these effects by making a breadwinner economically inessential.) Thus we have here a rich field for generating positive externalities—that is, for moderating the negative external effects just cited—through the device of low-wage subsidies. The sum total of these external effects, especially when the benefits to future generations are added, is perhaps the most important single external benefit to be expected from the proposed subsidy system. It is a recipe for renewed economic development in the ghettos and barrios of our inner cities.

Of what interest is it to today's citizens, other than disadvantaged parents themselves, that in the next generation the children of these parents will be more productive as a result of the subsidies and in the subsequent generations their grandchildren will also be more productive? These productivity improvements transmitted to future generations will ultimately lift up the productivity of the labor force in general or, more broadly, improve social conditions for a general benefit; and today's citizens will be willing to pay something, at least a partial contribution, toward these future improvements for the sake of their own children, who will be the direct beneficiaries. Surely there is something in this line of argument. But it is one of the most problematic of the external benefits to evaluate. As a shot in the dark, we might pick a number like $5 billion a year as what the taxpaying populace would be willing to pay out of their pockets and feel, in view of the external benefit accruing to their children, no worse off.

Another way of financing such an investment in disadvantaged children could be contemplated. Poor areas could be offered the same financial opportunities for self-help that third-world countries are offered. The government could run as a development bank, issuing long-term bonds with which to finance this generation's employment subsidies. To pay the interest on this debt over each future generation the bank could, it might be imagined, be given authority to levy a small payroll tax on the income of low-wage workers in future generations. Thus the children, on reaching the labor force, would themselves pay for the benefits accruing to them from their improved upbringing. Yet such a scheme of self-development might not be seen as entirely fair. Some of the children reaching the labor force in the next generation might miss out on a better upbringing or somehow fail to benefit from it, and it would be impracticable to limit the cost-sharing to the main beneficiaries.

Other Neighborhood Effects

When a person faces a very low relative wage and long waits before winning a job, self-reliance and self-respect are sorely tested. Some may lack the emotional strength to avoid falling into drug use, poor nutritional habits (worse than those required by their low income), and criminal activity such as drug dealing. Various hospital costs and property losses are imposed on others.

In urban areas with a high concentration of poverty, people's dim prospects for employment and pay also have the external effect of instilling the expectations of those prospects in others, even if their chances are better—or would be if they prepared for them. The larger the numbers who are unemployed or low paid, the poorer the odds will seem to others that their initiative and effort in their own careers will pay off. Where long spells between jobs and low wages are the rule, a culture of poverty is apt to grow up alongside the traditional culture—a culture distinguished by drugs, crime, and violence. The rest of the community and the rest of society pay much of the immediate cost, and there is also the cost of the defensive measures they have to take to hold down the total cost.

The system of low-wage employment subsidies will have the important benefit of reducing some of these costs to others. First of all, in raising pay and reducing waiting time for a job, the subsidies would have the "multiplier effect" of alleviating the pessimism and poor preparation that tend to spread like a contagion in poor communities, which would raise wages another notch. As a consequence the subsidy system would not have to be built on quite the scale that would otherwise be required.

As the culture of poverty is weakened, the costs to society of medical care and law enforcement will also be reduced. These benefits include, at the very least, the resulting savings in the budgetary outlay needed to yield the same level of health and public safety that existed before the subsidy system was put into place.

Since the Medicaid program now costs taxpayers more than $100 billion annually, it is a plausible guess that the reduced drug use and improved nutrition that could be expected to result from the subsidy system would provide a budgetary saving of $15 billion a year. The expense of the criminal justice system has also reached monumental proportions. Even as recently as 1988, expenditures for police protection ran about $26 billion, correction cost $19 billion, and the other judicial and legal services came to about $10 billion. These costs now total roughly $75 billion annually. It seems reasonable to suppose that the massive subsidy system proposed here would reduce the cost of achieving the current level of public safety by some $25 billion a year. Since most of these outlays are made by state and local governments, these budgetary savings could be made available to the federal government to offset some of the cost of employment subsidies only through an arrangement with the states.

Finally, the employment subsidies would have budgetary effects on the other programs of the welfare system. The low wages and high unemployment of the less productive members of society create a raft of negative external effects by adding to the number of people who, without some sort of safety net, would suffer economic distress—distress that would be manifested in increased begging, prostitution, and crime. The cost of operating this welfare system, not including Medicaid (already considered) and unemployment insurance benefits (to be considered), reached in 1990 a level close to $90 billion (in 1995 dollars). The low-wage employment subsidies would produce some important budgetary savings here.

With more single mothers on AFDC and related programs able to support themselves (or come close to it) as a result of the employment subsidies, fewer of them will qualify for welfare. Perhaps even more important, with more young men able to function again as providers, still fewer mothers will be eligible for

AFDC and related benefits. So large budgetary savings will result quite automatically from the low-wage employment subsidies. If we take the budgetary outlay of the proposed subsidy system to be $120 billion a year in the mid-1990s, it is not too much to expect that outlays for the AFDC program alone (leaving aside the allied programs for which its beneficiaries become eligible) would decline by $10 billion a year—a halving of the current outlay.

The recent shift of welfare management to the states, with its introduction of limits on the length of support, will begin to realize some budgetary saving in advance of the introduction of the subsidies. But it is clear that the planned limits will be problematic, and perhaps go unenforced, if no employment subsidies are put in place.

The principle can be extended to other allied parts of the welfare system. Title 20 social services for child care and housing benefits, together amounting to as much as AFDC, could also be expected to decline by half—by another $10 billion a year. Food stamp costs, also running about the same amount, might likewise drop by $10 billion. Supplemental Security Income, some of it going to working-age people suffering from disabilities, and General Assistance provided by localities for the needy, together totaling close to the same amount, might be expected to decline by $5 billion a year. So these parts of the welfare system, even without any tightening of eligibility rules, might see annual budgetary savings of some $35 billion.

All together, then, we have savings amounting to $75 billion a year. Again, not every billion is a saving for the federal government budget; some of it constitutes savings for state and local governments. But unquestionably the federal government could reach an agreement providing for some sort of cost sharing whereby it could recoup savings created by its employment subsidy program.

Effects on Tax Revenues

Most unemployment can be said to be involuntary. Those workers in the pool of the unemployed would be willing to accept a lower wage if it would lead to quick hiring, but the employers have their own reasons of employee incentive for requiring a higher wage. So the wage is said to be too high to "clear the market," and the unemployment pool is not absorbed by the firms. Without any such unemployment at all, with nothing to deter employees from quitting and shirking to their heart's delight, the enterprises would falter. But there is too much of this unemployment, since firms setting their wage above the market-clearing level do not take into account the effect on other firms (who must then raise their own wage still higher); and employees, in making their quitting and shirking decisions, do not take into account the effect on the reputation of employees everywhere.

The employment subsidy plan will bring a big improvement here by boosting employment and thus cut into this excessive unemployment. The direct—and main—beneficiaries are the low-wage workers, whose employment and earnings are increased. To raise tax rates on their earned income sufficiently to make them finance their own subsidies would erase much of the benefit, thus setting back the purpose of the plan. However, their gain will automatically create some budgetary savings for the government. With spells of unemployment of shorter duration, outlays for unemployment insurance benefits will be reduced; and, with employment higher, larger payments of unemployment insurance premiums will result. If unemployment rates return to the levels seen in the 1960s, it is reasonable to assume that the average annual outlay for unemployment benefits will likewise return to the level of that time, hence drop by about $6 billion; and premiums received will rise by $2 billion, for a total annual gain of $8 billion.

Two other revenue gains should be mentioned. One is the federal tax revenue from the increased corporate profits generated by the increased employment and associated increase of output and sales. This might be estimated at about $4 billion yearly.[4] The other is the increase in proceeds from state and local sales taxes. If we were to add in all the other miscellaneous levies we might arrive at another $3 billion yearly. Thus this area of external benefit arising from the employment subsidy system can be expected to generate additional government revenues of about $15 billion a year.

So far, then, an estimated annual total of $90 billion in budgetary savings and additional tax receipts has been identified.

The Earned Income Tax Credit

There is already in place a system of wage subsidies in the form of the Earned Income Tax Credit (EITC). Readers may be wondering why it would not be better simply to expand that program or build on it, rather than begin anew. The reverse is true. It would be best to close the EITC program, declaring that its most valuable benefits would be provided by the low-wage employment subsidies. The resulting annual savings would be a huge addition to the budgetary savings and tax receipts attributable to the subsidy plan.

The program was conceived as a way to offset the burden of payroll taxes on low-wage people. What evolved is a system of tax credits going directly to persons with low wage income. The credit is set at a flat rate up to a ceiling: each dollar of an eligible person's wage earnings brings in a credit—36¢—until the credit reaches a cap around $3,110. (This is more than enough to offset payroll and all other taxes due if nonwage income is comparably low, and the unused part of the credit is "refundable" in cash.) If virtually all taxpayers were to receive such a tax credit the budgetary cost to the federal government would be staggering—close to $400 billion a year. So the credit is designed to taper off with income once it exceeds some threshold around $11,300: for every dollar of wage income above that point, 20¢ of the credit is lost, until it is all gone.

Some commentators criticize this program for enhancing the reward to work of low-productivity workers without regard to any nonwage income the beneficiaries may have. But the criticism misses the point of boosting the reward to poorly paid work. The proper objective, whether the method is the present tax credits to low-wage workers or the proposed subsidies to firms for their employment, is not to lessen the degree of inequality in incomes.

It is to enable low-productivity workers to support themselves through their own labor, even though persons having high non-wage incomes might not need to do so, because earning one's way is valuable to people, *and* to encourage self-help and participation through employment in the legitimate business of the economy because for most people such a life is necessary to personal development and to the sense of belonging and contributing.

The real defects of the EITC lie elsewhere in its poor design. This program is not really a tool to reward and stimulate the employment of *low-wage workers* so much as a program of credits for those who, for whatever reason, have low *wage incomes*—and not over a lifetime but in the current year. Thus much of the credits is paid to people whose low wage income is simply the result of late entry or early withdrawal from the labor force. Furthermore, because the credit tapers off so slowly, eligible earners are due a tax credit until their earnings in the year reach $27,000, which considerably exceeds the median annual wage income.

The program is also quite poorly designed from the standpoint of its incentive effects on the behavior of low-wage people. Some of those able to earn $7 an hour or more who would have worked most of the year without the credit and who now find themselves receiving the ceiling credit of $3,110 with room to spare, may be tempted by it to work less—until doing so begins to cost a loss of the credit. An objective of policy here should be to *raise* employment, not lower it. Second, consider those workers whose productivity is so low that, with intermittent joblessness as a result of layoffs and occasional quitting and an hourly wage around $4 or $5, their wage income might average around $5,000 a year. For them, the 36 percent tax credit amounts to only $1,800—or $1.53 an hour. That is nothing like the transformative increase envisaged by the proposed subsidy program for low-wage employment, which would raise a $4 wage to around $7. The worst defect of the EITC is that it encourages *least* the employment of those whose job attachment and capacity for self-help are weakest.

Finally, the EITC program has, from its inception, labored under the bizarre restriction that, until very recently, its eligible beneficiaries were only the wage-earner(s) in families with dependent children. As a result, the program perversely neglects the problems raised by low wages and unemployment where they are most acute—among men, especially young men who lack the economic prospects to marry and raise children. In supplementing the earnings of single heads of family, very few of whom are men, the program may very well operate, as the welfare system must surely operate, to make it less advantageous for these women to marry. Furthermore, insofar as men or women with dependent children are encouraged by the tax credit to supply their labor more steadily, they may to some extent drive down the market wage. To this extent the program adds to the division of society between those who have ample incentive to work and those who do not.

If the proposed employment subsidies are enacted, the poor design of the EITC and the inadequacy of even its ceiling benefits will stick out like a sore thumb. A fine way of obtaining the remaining financing, therefore, would be to close the EITC program and credit the savings to the new subsidy program. The budgetary cost of the EITC is now approaching $35 billion per year. When that budgetary saving is added to the previous sum, the total reaches $120 billion.

The total of estimated tax revenues and budgetary savings attributable to the employment subsidies plan is in the neighborhood of the budgetary cost of the plan, approximately $125 billion, as explained earlier. One may say that the plan would finance itself—a little more, perhaps, or a little less.

Nevertheless the plan has another set of external benefits. Their existence could justify the collection of some further tax revenue in case it is ever estimated that the subsidy plan is short of financing itself from the sources discussed above.

Responsibility toward Our Collaborators in Production

The economist Kenneth Arrow suggests that the members of a society sense an implicit social contract setting forth some rights and responsibilities toward one another:

One way of looking at ethics and morality . . . is that these principles are agreements, conscious or, in many cases, unconscious, to supply mutual benefits . . . Societies in their evolution have developed implicit agreements to certain kinds of regard for others, agreements which are essential to the survival of society or at least contribute greatly to the efficiency of its working.[5]

It is increasingly agreed in discussions of jurisprudence and moral philosophy, however, that people's feeling of responsibility toward others is contingent upon the nature of their relationship to the particular others in question. The structure of who is doing what with whom matters for how a person is treated.

A sense of responsibility toward others is often observed among those who are engaged in some sort of joint effort—the company where we work, the army, or even the national economy we enter on reaching working age. With Sam Spade's line in *The Maltese Falcon,* "When someone kills your partner, you have to do something about it," we understand that even tough guys with gravel voices feel a reciprocal responsibility toward their associates and, more generally, those in society with whom they cooperate, directly or indirectly. "Deep inside," a recent letter to the editor of the *Financial Times* put it, "we are programmed against certain kinds of action. Thus, when someone falls seriously behind, we slow down and extend a hand—irrespective of the context."[6] Europeans regularly pay tribute to these values with the words "solidarity" and "social cohesion." The economist Arthur Okun saw an "invisible handshake" within the working population that has a place alongside Adam Smith's "invisible hand" of the marketplace.[7] These feelings may not be as strong as the obligation felt toward siblings and other blood relatives, which sociobiologists attribute to our genes. Fortunately, though, even the most exacting standard of economic justice does not require that we risk our lives for our fellow workers in the national economy—only that we risk some dollars.

On this view, there is a fourth external benefit that would accrue to the rest of the labor force from instituting low-wage employment subsidies. In acting through the government to pull up the rewards and thus to stimulate the participation and employment of low-wage workers, the more fortunate members of the labor force would be removing a source of some embarrassment. The more advantaged in society would gain pride and self-respect from the sense of having met their end of the social contract—of having acted justly. If so, they will be willing to pay something to achieve this satisfaction in the form of higher taxes—on their paychecks or their total incomes. If, further, what people are willing to pay for this benefit and the other external benefits from the low-wage subsidy system is enough to cover the budgetary cost of the system, that is ample reason to enact it.

There are dissenters to this view. The free-market economists deny that it is right or just that any worker should be rewarded by society with more than his or her productivity. The most famous expressions in this vein are from Friedrich Hayek, the renowned economic theorist and political philosopher. He exposes the silliness of several proposed alternatives to the productivity criterion for pay: that pay ought to be equal for all (then the state, to implement such an order, would need to abridge the right of equal treatment—"equality before the law"—to those advantaged by nature or nurture); that the productivity criterion is fair only when all have the "same start" on reaching adulthood (then all students would have to be restricted to the same course of study or one deemed equivalent); that a worker's pay should depend on the "moral merit" of his or her preparation (then the state would reward the failures of diligent incompetents and not reward the efforts it cannot observe); and that mere "membership in a particular . . . nation entitles the individual to a particular material standard that is determined by the general wealth of the group" (then by analogy poor countries would have the similar right to a share of the wealth of the world economy).[8]

However, Hayek fails to recognize a long-accepted tenet of orthodox economics: just as the yield on land benefits from a supply of labor to till it and the productivity of labor benefits from land to till, so the productivity of workers advantaged in talent or skill benefits from the supply of less advantaged workers and vice-versa. The cooperation of two or more "types" of workers—either collaboration shoulder-to-shoulder or simply the coordination of their respective activities—yields a gain in their aggregate product, or income, over the sum of what they could produce and earn as two or more separate nations. (The gain mostly arises from the differences between the "nations" just as the gain from trade between two countries largely arises from their differences.) This gain—this surplus from cooperation—clearly makes it possible for every class of worker to gain from the cooperation or for some class or classes to gain while the others hold their own. How these gains are in fact distributed depends upon prevailing taxes, subsidies, and so forth.

The surplus generated by economic cooperation—the cooperation of types or of individual workers—is the starting point in contemporary thinking about economic justice (or distributive justice in the older term). This is made most explicit by the philosopher John Rawls, who regards the "subject" of justice as the "division of the advantages from social cooperation."[9] It provides the basic question for debate: How should subsidies and taxes "tilt" in view of their effect on how this surplus is distributed?

Once we view the marketplace in this light, we have to part company with those free-market advocates who oppose any low-wage subsidy as a matter of principle, no matter what the distributive outcome is without one. To oppose such a subsidy in principle is to believe that the market will always be right in how it causes the surplus to be distributed, without any assistance from low-wage subsidies. Few will deem it satisfactory if, when the less advantaged have a productivity so low that they cannot afford a lifestyle remotely like that further up the scale, the market is found to be funneling all or most of the surplus to the more advantaged. In the event of such an extreme outcome it would be natural to ask how to move more of the surplus over to the less advantaged.

Of course Hayek, with Milton Friedman and many others in the classical-liberal tradition, have instead favored welfare support for those in extreme poverty—"for the weak or the infirm or for the victims of unforeseeable disaster."[10] But this reply fails to see that adequate welfare mixed with inadequate wages fuels feelings of powerlessness and desperation, leading to idleness and dependency, and possibly drugs, crime, and violence.

Another product of free-market thinking is a recent amendment to the idea of a "flat tax" championed by Jack Kemp. Personal income below some threshold would be exempted from the flat rate. But that would be a feeble step toward any major improvement in the reward to less productive labor, since the problems created by wages of $5 or even $8 an hour are not met by exempting what little can be earned at that wage from a 20 percent tax. And it would be extremely inefficient, since middle- and high-income people, of whom there are a great number, would then also pay nothing on their first $10,000 or $16,000, whatever the threshold was; so tax rates would have to be increased in the higher brackets, with serious effects on effort, saving, investment, and entrepreneurship. Finally, the low-income exemption would spread its tax breaks to persons with low wealth and middle wages as much as to persons with low wages and middle wealth, and thus would set us back to thinking always of income and never of the crucial importance of work and its reward.

If, as I will suggest below, the more advantaged do tend, when there are no low-wage subsidies for the less productive, to receive an appreciable share of the surplus, what would be a fairer way to allot it? What say the philosophers who have contributed to thinking about justice in the rewards to collaborative effort? They have not all taken the same path, of course. But there is one line of thinking, which came into prominence three decades ago, that stands out for its clarity and operational character—and, for many of us, whether or not we go all the way with it, its moral appeal.

In this view, a fair shake among cooperating parties would reapportion (wholly or partially) the share of the surplus that the more advantaged found themselves with—delivering the maximum amount possible to the less advantaged. (There is no risk that doing so would leave the less productive paid worse than the more productive, since the latter will always retain an edge.) If that costs the more productive all the surplus they had, they still do not lose, though neither do they gain—the others obtain the whole of the gain. If after the more productive have delivered as much surplus as they can they have some left over, then they gain. This justice is not like charity, and the case for it does not invoke the motives people have for occasional acts of charity. If the more fortunate act according to this sense of justice, it is not that they have such delicate sensibilities that they cannot stand to see inequality; they may be quite capable of shrugging off some awful inequalities. It is because they would feel they were doing something ugly, something that would make them feel less good about themselves, less proud of themselves, if they insisted not merely on having their old wage, the wage they earned before cooperation, but in addition on retaining part of the surplus as a sort of surcharge for their cooperation with their less advantaged partners.[11]

This notion of fairness is very old. A familiar example is the two people who can enjoy a cake—their surplus—if they can agree on how to share it. The solution considered fair is to let the disadvantaged one cut the cake into two pieces with the understanding that the advantaged one will have his choice and take the larger piece. This arrangement ensures that the reward to the disadvantaged—the smaller of the two pieces—is as large as possible.[12] But this image directs us to thinking of equal shares, which is a wrong turn. It is best to think of the advantaged as the cake baker, who will willingly pay the cost of baking a bigger cake the larger is the relative share that the cake cutter offers him.

Ayn Rand, the Russian-born novelist-philosopher usually located terrifyingly far to the right on the political spectrum, evoked the image of a bus, operated and maintained by the more fortunate, in which the less fortunate ride free—subsidized tickets on a space-available basis. The more fortunate pass up any part of the gains from cooperation with the less fortunate, content with the same benefit net of cost from the operation of the bus that they would have obtained without cooperation. By analogy, a society that reflected on the matter would arrange subsidies so that disadvantaged workers, to the extent practicable, were rewarded with the whole of the surplus generated by their contribution to the market economy.[13]

John Rawls's thesis is rooted in production economies with collaborative employment. The more advantaged, if they think about the matter in a properly impartial way, will not want any part of their gain from cooperation with others to come at the expense of the less advantaged. Since the market (before any subsidies) places some of the surplus with the more advantaged, the more advantaged must tax themselves to finance subsidies that will deliver to the less advantaged the largest possible part of the surplus—to provide them with the greatest possible gain from the cooperation. Rawls focuses on the strong possibility that the fiscal instruments have sufficiently distortionary side effects on people's incentives that when the maximum possible amount of surplus has been delivered to the less advantaged, the more advantaged have left some share of the surplus—so they gain from the cooperation as well as the less advantaged.

This is the best feasible arrangement for the less advantaged. The subsidies do not erase the difference in their wage rates,[14] but the inequality in wage rates is *in the service of the disadvantaged*. If cries of envy from the less advantaged were to pressure society into still heavier tax rates on the more advantaged, the after-tax wage of the latter would fall but *so would the wage of the less advantaged*—though not by nearly as much. Wage "inequality" (both the absolute and percentage differences between the two wage rates) would be reduced, but it would be a hollow victory for those among the less advantaged who valued a higher reward. (Rawls does not consider the possibility that, even if inequality is reduced to what makes the absolute wage of the less advantaged as high as possible, these low earners are suffering from their low *relative* wage. He might say that even the more advantaged have rights.)[15]

The nineteenth-century utilitarians take a different view. The upshot, though, is not very different. They would not require the more advantaged to arrange the maximum possible reward to the less advantaged. But they would move in that direction and might come close.

It is plausible to believe, then, that the public and its representatives, on grasping this respected line of philosophical thinking, would agree to a redistribution of some portion of the more productive workers' share of the surplus—through a flat payroll tax rate, say, used to finance increased low-wage subsidies—on the proviso that the increased rates yield increased tax revenue, of course, and the further proviso that the increased subsidies be effective in raising wages and employment among the less advantaged. Their resulting feeling that in taking this collective action they are relinquishing an unjust share of the surplus from cooperation is a sort of external benefit to them from the agreed subsidy program.

In that case, we want to estimate the amount of the surplus from cooperation that the market apportions to the more productive—or, rather, what that portion would be if the less advantaged were fully reenlisted in the market economy. The numerical analysis of illustrative, stylized examples of production economies is fairly convincing that the percentage gain in the average wage rate of the more productive is not very large—not 50 percent, or 25, and possibly not even 10 percent. After all, it is not as if some production is greatly facilitated by labor inputs that are uniquely provided by disadvantaged workers; advantaged workers can do that work too. Another factor is the very high productivity of the more productive relative to that of the less productive, a ratio of around 3. (Furthermore, the advantaged do not need the disadvantaged to do various low-skill jobs if they can import the goods produced by such workers; but this factor has been held aside.) A ballpark estimate of the percentage gain is 1 percent; it may be more than three times that or less than one-third that, but it seems a good bet that the correct number is inside that range.[16] If we take the "more productive" to be the upper half of the workers in the earnings distribution and assume they earn three-quarters of the wage bill, their earnings are running about $3 trillion a year. A 1 percent gain in those earnings amounts, then, to $30 billion a year.

This conservative estimate puts the illustrative low-wage employment subsidy program well over the top. When the previously calculated sum of budgetary savings and additional tax proceeds generated by the program, $100 billion per year, is added to the $30 billion estimated to be gained by the more productive from their cooperation with the less productive, the total actually exceeds the estimate of the budgetary cost of the program, which is around $110 billion or, if the stimulus to employment is figured in, around $125 billion a year.

Before we leave the matter of financing, there is a further point. Once wage rates and employment levels among the less advantaged have been raised by the wage subsidy system, there is no longer a rationale, other than historical accident, for exempting low incomes from income tax. Why not reinstate the old income tax rates on low incomes and the modest exemption levels of old, and earmark some of the resulting revenues to boost wage subsidies further to compensate for the tax increase and use the rest to ease tax rates in the middle and higher brackets, thus to compensate middle-income people for the higher levy on their first few thousands of income and to stimulate entrepreneurship and investment by high-income people? If even a mere five points were added to the income tax rate on all income below the median level, there would be a bountiful increase of tax revenues—some $50 billion in proceeds from those in the lower half of the income distribution, whose total income must run well over $1 trillion, and another $50 billion from the equal number of persons in the upper half of the distribution.

But such a suggestion runs against the worrying new trend in political circles: to concentrate the federal income tax on the top half of the income distribution, which will leave the tax rates in the high brackets much too high, as now, or will require a further shrinkage of the federal government to the point where it must default on some core missions—including, quite possibly, the expenditures and subsidies needed to defend the country from the forces of disintegration and disorder at home.

To conclude: the employment subsidies would soon generate budgetary savings and additional tax receipts that would roughly cover the budgetary cost of the program. However, the external benefits would be even greater. For example, the budgetary saving in crime prevention would be equal to the reduction in outlays consistent with an unchanged crime rate. But this reduction would generally be less than the total external benefit of the reduced propensity to commit crime achieved by the subsidies, since the taxpayers would have the valuable choice of spending more to reduce crime or of accepting some increase in crime to reduce crime-prevention outlays further. There are also other external benefits that do not generate an automatic budgetary inflow but that are valuable nonetheless, such as the satisfaction of extending to our collaborators in the nation's economic activity what we deem to be a fair shake. The subsidy system would therefore produce a net positive gain for taxpayers.

10

.

The Flaws in Other Approaches

The proposal to introduce subsidies for low-wage employment
has to compete against other proposals. A system of low-wage
employment subsidies has all the markings of an economist's idea,
and it is that. The great British public finance scholar Arthur Cecil
Pigou, with his work in the interwar period, was the first economist of distinction to analyze the effects of "wage subsidies." In
1935 the Hungarian-born theorist Nicholas Kaldor proposed employment subsidies to assist the United States and Britain to recover from their lingering depression.[1] Kaldor's thesis was that a
subsidy system would very nearly pay for itself, the same conclusion I reached in Chapter 9. These analyses both took a nonmone-
tary view of employment and wages. When Keynes convinced the
economics profession that most of the unemployment in that
period was due to monetary phenomena—"deficient effective demand"—the idea of wage subsidies fell out of fashion, if not into
disrepute. Then, when economists concluded that the usual monetary maladjustment works itself out—that unemployment tends
toward its current "natural" level, through wage adjustments or
the traditional behavior of the central bank—the way was clear
for a return of the idea of employment subsidies.

The massive rise in structural unemployment, and thus in the
level of unemployment to which the economy tends to settle
down, has stimulated interest in the feasibility, costs, and benefits

of employment subsidies. In Britain the labor economist Richard Layard has led a team of researchers exploring the effects of wage subsidies (and of unemployment benefits) on the natural level of unemployment and the associated wage rates.[2] In this country there was early work by Daniel Hammermesh, Robert Haveman, and James Palmer.[3] The present decade has seen new work by Dennis Snower and by Hian Teck Hoon and me.[4] A number of figures in labor economics have published comparisons of the various kinds of plans.[5]

Yet there seems to be resistance to the idea. Why? In part it is a suspicion that the budgetary cost will be enormous and doubt that the budgetary savings and revenues generated will make most of it up. In part it is also fear of the unknown—a leap into not fully charted waters. More important are the objections that, while a low-wage subsidy might be effective, there exists a *better* way. Indeed, many better ways, since these opponents are dispersed over distinct camps, each one far from the others.

To persuade people of the wisdom of proceeding with low-wage employment subsidies, it is necessary to show that these alternative approaches are deficient for hitting the target to be aimed at, whatever may be their advantages as means to other ends. It is impossible to take up all of them, though. I will look at the deficiency or deficiencies in a selection of these programs, actual or proposed.

The Statutory Minimum Wage

This instrument originated in Australasia and reached the United States in 1933 as part of the National Industrial Recovery Act. The Supreme Court struck down the act in 1935 but reversed itself 1937, opening the way for the Fair Labor Standards Act of 1938. This law established a nationwide minimum hourly wage and fixed a premium for overtime hours.

If the purpose of the law is to curb, or cut, employment at wage rates below the statutory rate, there is no serious dispute about its effectiveness. While there continue to be jobs paying below the legal minimum, they are driven underground where they are harder for workers to find and they pose hazards to those taking them. Employment at wages below the minimum has thus been reduced. Critics of the law say that in this respect it is all too effective: some people badly wanted those jobs and are denied them by the law.

Controversy over the effects of the minimum wage on employment continues to this day. Defenders of a statutory minimum pooh-pooh the effects on employment. Standard economic analysis opens the door a crack to such a cheerful prognosis: There is a possibility that an increase of the statutory minimum may, up to a point, actually increase employment. (Some employers may have held back on the jobs they offer to avoid driving up the local wage too much; when the law raises the wage in spite of their efforts there is no longer reason to hold back.) But standard doctrine equally predicts that an increase of the statutory minimum to a sufficiently high level is bound to decrease employment: all the affected workers would be priced out of the market. No economist I know of has suggested that wage rates of $4 an hour might be pushed up to $7 by means of a hike of the minimum wage without causing a major decline in employment among low-wage workers. There are scraps of evidence that raising the minimum wage does cause such a decline.

There are also reasons for believing that even if employers, in the face of a mandated wage increase, maintain their employment of their current low-wage employees, in whom they have invested something, they will look for ways to get along with fewer of them as these employees eventually move on. The long-run effects might be much larger, therefore, than those detected early on.

As a result of the decreased availability of employment, the waiting time between jobs, already undesirably long, would be lengthened further. For those low-wage workers with strong job attachment, the wage increase achieved might be judged worth the unemployment cost, at least if there was some confidence that the spells of joblessness would be widely shared on a sort of rotating basis. But for those workers with tenuous job attachment or the likelihood of frequent job loss, the longer wait might not be worth the increased wage. They might not be able to weather long spells of unemployment as easily as those in more stable or more comfortable situations. One of the more securely established facts in this area is that *prolonged* bouts of unemployment are linked to rates of mental illness, hospital admission rates, alcoholism, and severe depression.

Even if an increase in the minimum wage is considered a net gain, it is a second-best solution. The program of employment subsidies outlined here is a preferable way to achieve higher pay at the low-wage end of the labor market since it would solve the problem of low wages without adding to the unemployment problem. Indeed it would pull employment up, not down. Since all of this is perfectly standard analysis, available from any quarter of the economics profession, it is impossible to understand the lingering appeal of the statutory minimum wage as a way to widen self-support, social cohesion, and so on among the disadvantaged.[6]

Public-Sector Jobs

Many black leaders continue to believe that increased public-sector employment of low-wage workers would boost black wages and employment. But it will not help much simply to create more public-sector jobs, with their competitive pay, in a poor area. The impact on unemployment in the targeted area may at first be favorable, as some of the new vacancies are filled from the local unemployment pool rather than from residents employed in the private sector. This effect on the unemployment rate will dwindle, however, since private employers in the area will allow their workforce to shrink once they notice that their employees' performance and job attachment have declined with the increased tightness of the labor market. Their labor costs will return to normal only when the local unemployment rate is more or less where it was before. Thus the mere substitution of public-sector jobs for private-sector jobs will not serve to reduce the natural unemployment rate in the area.

Creating premium-paying public-sector positions carrying super-competitive job security or amenities is apt to make conditions *worse*. When private employment has shrunk by enough to push the unemployment rate back to where it was before the new super-jobs, a problem will become visible: everyone will be attracted by the thought of landing one of those jobs. As a result, employee loyalty and performance are apt not to be fully restored by the reestablishment of the old unemployment rate. Private firms will be more cautious about training new recruits because of the risk that employees will leave for jobs in the public sector. This is like the eastern German disease—the siren call of a high-paid job in the west stands in the way of high job attachment in the east and willingness to take a lower-paid job that would accelerate employment recovery and capital investment in the east. Thus, subsidies to a small anointed sub-set of employers, in this case some government agencies, serve to raise pay for those workers who land one of these specially attractive jobs; that reduces job attachment at private firms, raising their labor costs; and that in turn raises the unemployment rate.

Just as the ill effect of the minimum wage on employment can be corrected only with compensatory employment subsidies, so the ill effect of creating a privileged cache of super-competitive public-sector jobs can be remedied only by employment subsidies for the private sector in order to create a balancing increase in the employability of workers in that sector. But, again, once such subsidies have been introduced through the broad private sector, where most of the jobs are, there is little reason to keep any similar subsidies for public agencies. The purpose of the subsidies is to permit the broadest possible integration of disadvantaged workers into the business of society, which is the activity of the private sector.

Growth

If we are concerned about workers' wages, many business people say, we ought to focus more on doing all we can to increase economic growth. It is true that the strains and injustices of life are a great deal easier to bear when we are becoming rich and successful at a rapid rate. And, historically, growth of the economy's total output per manhour worked has usually promoted growth of wages as well. Wages have usually maintained a roughly steady share of the rising output—though this share can shift to a higher plateau or, as in the present era, a lower one.

The thesis that growth is especially good for less advantaged workers rests on the belief that their relative share of the current rewards to work is higher the faster average productivity per worker is growing. This thesis is plausible. It was precisely when economic growth shifted to a slower pace in the mid-1970s that the gap between wage rates at the low end of the scale and those in the middle started widening to its current size and unemployment rates at the low end of the labor market began their steep climb to their present level.

However, to go from viewing slower growth as *a* cause of the worsened situation of the disadvantaged to seeing faster growth as *the* cure is a big step. First, the slowdown in growth was one of several shocks, temporary and permanent, that struck the economy in the past two decades. There are no estimates of the size of its effect. No evidence has been offered on the usual effect of technological advance on the relative wage of workers of particular backgrounds and talents.

Second, there would be huge risks if the government took measures to speed economic growth as a solution to the dual problem of a low relative wage and disproportionate joblessness among the low-paid. An initiative to speed up growth would require doing particular things, such as legislating investment tax credits to spur capital formation by American corporations. These particular thrusts might or might not help raise relative wages and employment in the lower part of the earnings distribution. Initiatives to speed growth directed instead at stimulating technological advance might boost the demand for the more educated workers, who could handle the more rapid pace of change, and grease the skids of those who couldn't.

Lastly, it is not appreciated how enormous the economic forces must be to alter the long-term rate of productivity growth by as little as a quarter of a percentage point. The fact that the great slowdown is worldwide, and far greater in many other countries, suggests that resuming the rapid growth of the postwar decades would be a Herculean task.

The conclusion is not that economic growth should be discouraged. The right policy is to accompany technological advance with low-wage employment subsidies so that low-wage workers do not become casualties in its path. Only in that way can there be any confidence that the gain from economic growth will be shared with the less advantaged.

Training and Education

A new school of thought holds that the best way to remedy the plight of the low-paid is through improved and extended education. The key is to help them increase their productivity by offering them the education and vocational training needed to understand and utilize the constantly more sophisticated technologies.

The devil is in the details, though. Training for what? And decided by whom? Nonexperts tend to assume that there are experts capable of foreseeing what kinds of skills will be in demand a decade or more into the future, but economists have never felt able to do that. It shows a profound lack of understanding of capitalism to suppose that outsiders can anticipate the training that entrepreneurs can make use of before the entrepreneurs have decided what goods or services they will try to sell and what methods of production they will try. Decisions about most training are best made by the entrepreneurs, while workers are best placed to decide about their education.

The other question is the kind of institutional arrangement to be set up to provide the desired training. Inevitably thoughts turn to Germany's "dual system" of vocational training, which combines vocational school coursework with a program of apprentice-training in a workplace paid for by the enterprise. But this system is an integral part of a network of occupations and standards that go back in some cases to the medieval guild system and that enjoy the protection and support of strong labor unions and extensive oversight by government. In the United States more jobs are created by new firms and employers are not required to provide as much job security. Ironically, just when admiration for the German system is growing strong, the Germans are rethinking it. Hit by many of the economic shocks felt in the United States and, in addition, the new competition from nearby Eastern Europe, western Germany saw the unemployment rate among its less educated workers double between the late 1970s and the late 1980s—a record no better than that of the United States.

The call for training also overlooks the huge size of the increase in the productivity of low-wage workers that would be needed to restore its relative level to its position of the late 1970s, when even absolute (not just relative) wages started to slide. What would this cost? The answer depends on the productivity, or effectiveness, of the training or education per dollar—that is, the return on the expenditure made. Careful evaluations of the effect on earnings of the many experimental training programs of the federal and state governments have yielded a wide range of estimated returns— from quite good returns from training of welfare recipients to negligible or even negative returns on the training of disadvantaged youth.[7] An evaluation of British experiments with so-called active labor market policies concludes that the programs are "decidedly uninspiring," and notes that "there can be a price to pay for exaggerating the role of labor market programs, if it leads to the neglect of other policy instruments."[8]

In a celebrated paper on the cost of the training required to restore low wages, the economist James Heckman cuts through the problematic evaluations of the myriad experimental programs by making a simple assumption: "[To] add $1,000 in earnings per year to the average person it is necessary to make a one-time investment of $10,000 in that person"—that is, the rate of return is 10 percent per year. He calculates that approximately $665 billion would have to be invested to restore the wages of high school dropouts and another $840 billion to restore the wages of high school graduates to their 1979 level—for a one-time total outlay in excess of $1.6 trillion.[9]

Would that investment, despite its stunning initial cost, be the best solution? This huge expense and the major institutional innovations that would be required to implement it raise awkward questions. It is unlikely that the program would go beyond addressing the earning power of school-age persons. Persons over thirty years old would not make it past the triage. And such a program could probably not be fully operating in less than a decade. It would take more than a generation until just one generation received the new training at full strength.

Another drawback is that, even if the entire $2 trillion outlay (expressed in, say, 1997 dollars rather than Heckman's 1989 dollars) could somehow be made at once, the subsequent annual interest and depreciation on that capital investment—as old workers die and have to be succeeded by trained replacements—might be around $120 billion, which is not significantly cheaper than the employment subsidy program. But this investment, in aiming at most to raise low-wage earnings by one-fifth or less, has a more modest goal than the subsidy program, which would raise $4 wages to about $7, for example. Furthermore, Heckman's assumed 10 percent rate of return is almost surely an overestimate; 5 percent would be more accurate.

The pessimistic view taken by Gilles Saint-Paul suggests another problem that may afflict the training approach. In this unfortunate case, the increased supply of workers trained to do word processing and spreadsheets reduces the cost of getting a letter typed or a table prepared; this is turn reduces the hourly wage at which employers will be willing to employ workers who lack the improved skills, as their productivity (always in value terms) is reduced.[10]

Finally, it is a legitimate question whether this approach, in the absence of wage subsidies, is likely to have broad success in reintegrating *very* disadvantaged workers—particularly those who have to contend with the norms that develop in high-poverty communities—into a society of self-support and job attachment. Such persons would have little interest in the programs of enriched education and extended training, and thus the programs would have little effectiveness, when the entire scale of wage rates that the students could hope to earn appeared too low to deserve their attention and energy. (The difference between a $6 wage and a $7 wage may be too small to energize them.) It is also difficult to create a classroom conducive to study when the students come from communities engulfed by problems caused by the failure of legitimate jobs to offer a living wage. It may be that the training route out of poverty is not practicable unless it is accompanied by employment subsidies.

I do not wish to be too negative, however. There are ways around the worst pitfalls of a training initiative, as some of the more sophisticated advocates have come to see. Suppose the government each year were to distribute to each able-bodied person of working age a voucher (worth thousands when redeemed) that could be exchanged with any private employer of his or her choice in return for a contract of employment for another year. The voucher might be viewed as defraying the recurring training that an employer must constantly provide employees in order to maintain or increase their usefulness. But what is such a scheme if not an employment subsidy in disguise? There is not much difference between such a scheme and the employment subsidy plan outlined in this book. One can view employment subsidies (and their cousins, hiring subsidies) as compensation for the training costs borne by employers.

The Morality of Responsibility and Respectability

The 1990s have seen an unexpected reemphasis on the importance of the bourgeois values of personal responsibility and respectability. I also have stressed the importance of self-reliance and steady work in the legitimate economy, both for their healthy effects on personal development and for their external effects on the rest of the community. Some new thinking seems to be going a great deal further, as in books by William Bennett and Gertrude Himmelfarb.[11]

The new thinking does not simply argue the *necessity* of a return to old-fashioned values. It asserts the *sufficiency* of right moral conduct as a means to economic development of the less advantaged. All the responsibility and respectability in the world will not alter the fact that the bottom third, say, of the earnings distribution must be occupied by somebody—by exactly one-third of the earners. As long as their productivity does not lift off to levels far above what has so far been seen in this country, they will not be able to afford the mainstream way of life, with its bourgeois values. Low-wage subsidies and those venerable values go together. Without the appreciation of those values there is no likelihood that we will see the enactment of low-wage employment subsidies. But without those subsidies a large minority of the population will not be able to live according to those values.

In contemplating these instruments and approaches, which are so inadequate and in many cases ill-suited to rid the economy of shamefully low wages and dangerously low employment among the disadvantaged, it would be easy to be cynical. One could see in each approach the pressure of some vested interest and the normal operation of what has been termed the politics of gesture.[12]

Another view is that everyone is subject to habits of mind. We are accustomed to a set of governmental instruments, and it is natural to ask how these instruments might best be readjusted when a new problem turns up. But readjusting old instruments is seldom the best way to respond. New problems usually demand new instruments for their solution. Wages offending the sense of decency brought forth minimum-wage legislation. Society's need for literacy and numeracy brought public subsidies for basic education. It is a perversion of these policy instruments to bend them toward purposes for which they are ill-suited and were never intended.

The new problem facing us today is that, from a social stand-point, work is now seriously undervalued by the marketplace, especially at the low end where the private reward to employment has fallen to a dangerous level. This new problem is best met with a new tool—subsidies that will pull up the private reward to work to a level that is congruent with its social worth.

11

·

Reply to Objections

In his book *The Rhetoric of Reaction: Perversity, Futility, Jeopardy,* Albert Hirschman finds a pattern in the attacks on every new progressive idea.[1] The jeopardy argument is that the innovation would endanger existing accomplishments or prospects; the perversity argument is that it would have unintended consequences leaving the intended beneficiaries worse off than before; the futility argument is that it would be ineffective in yielding the benefits promised.

Objections of each kind have been made against the idea of low-wage employment subsidies. Here I will attempt to rebut these objections, and, in doing so, provide a vision of the country that the employment subsidies would foster.

The Futility Objections

The most extreme futility thesis holds that low-wage employment subsidies will be effective in raising neither employment nor paychecks. Businessmen often give a modern argument for this proposition based on the importance of skills and the costliness of training the disadvantaged.

Today, it is argued, most of the work to be done requires skills. There may have been a time when unskilled workers could often do the work of a skilled worker if there were enough of them, so they could be hired if their cost per worker was a small enough fraction of the skilled worker's cost; now, however, unskilled workers would damage expensive equipment or distract valuable personnel to such an extent that their contribution would be nil or negative. So there is no substitute for training. But workers of limited talent or disadvantaged background, the argument goes, are not trainable or can be trained only at an exorbitant expense: no matter how much training time the employer invested in them, the results would fall short of repaying the investment. So even when trained for skilled jobs, their net productivity, after allowance for training costs, would still be zero or negative. Therefore, aside from the considerable number still employed for menial tasks, these less fortunate persons are not employable—and would not be even if subsidies reduced their hourly labor costs to zero.

There are several points of misunderstanding here. First, the low-wage subsidy plan does not aim to create jobs for unproductive workers. It offers its matching grants only to those an employer is willing to pay something out of his own pocket, in recognition of their productivity. To be accurate, it offers subsidies to employ those workers whose productivity, though low, is high enough that the hourly labor cost borne by their employer exceeds some threshold level—the level where the plan's matching grants kick in.

Second, the subsidies would offset some (if not all) of the cost of training the unskilled for more skilled work. Some of the unskilled, after all, would surely have come close to qualifying for that training even without the government's intervention, and the subsidies would put those workers over the top. Thus the employment subsidies can be expected to *widen* the set of workers who can profitably be placed in medium-skill jobs. In decreasing the labor costs of hiring those workers, the subsidy plan will draw more of those workers from unemployment or alternative pursuits into jobs.

Finally, the proposition that more hiring of unskilled workers requires training more unskilled workers for skilled work rests on a false premise: that the economy has only a fixed amount of unskilled work to be done, no matter how low the net hourly labor cost. In this lump-of-work view, employees of different skill levels have to work in virtually fixed proportions to one another, and the skilled workers are almost fully utilized already. So firms are already employing almost all the unskilled needed to complement the economy's supply of skilled workers. Subsidies reducing the cost of employing low-wage workers, in this view, could result in only a minuscule increase in unskilled employment, and the consequent tightening of the labor market would be so small as to yield only a small increase in these workers' pay. (A small increase in employment of all types of workers is made affordable by the reduced cost of low-wage workers.)

Is there evidence for the lump-of-work view? The finding of some investigators that this or that increase in the statutory minimum wage did not notably contract low-wage employment might be seen as indirect evidence for it. Seemingly it does not matter much to employers how much or how little the low-skill labor costs them. However, the previous chapter warned of the snares in this evidence: The short-run employment effects may not be very harmful; but the long-run employment effects of the minimum wage matter more, and these are far more deleterious, as producers adopt more labor-saving machinery in response to increased labor costs. And a small increase in a low-level minimum wage may actually be helpful, raising employment in isolated labor markets dominated by a few employers by removing their incentive to hold back their hiring to keep wages down; but a large increase in the minimum wage, of a size believed to make low-wage workers self-supporting, might price low-wage workers out of the market.

There is more direct evidence to consider. The lump-of-work view implies that, other factors unchanged, shoehorning even small numbers of the less productive into jobs requires a big cut in the hourly labor cost of employing them—and hence a big cut in their pay, absent increased subsidies or reduced taxes. International evidence does not bear out such a strong relationship, though: the relative wage of the unskilled is not particularly depressed in countries where the unskilled are a high proportion of the employed. (The United States is not a country with a massive proletariat and a tiny elite of college graduates, so the wage gap here cannot be explained along those lines.) Neither does the evidence across the 50 states of the union. The relative wage (relative to the median) of the less educated workers in a state does not show any systematic relationship to their number relative to the labor force in that state.[2] Other studies have also found that the wage within a given educational group is little influenced by the group's unemployment rate.[3]

These findings are almost too good to be true. They suggest that a substantial increase in the employment of a particular kind of worker would not have a negative effect on those workers' productivity—a virtual suspension of the law of diminishing returns. The reconciliation with standard thinking is that the global economy is very big. The productivity of a given type of worker might be driven down by a *massive* increase in the number of such workers employed in the global economy. But a 10 percent increase in the number of such workers in California or even in the national economy is not capable of having much of an effect on wages there or elsewhere. One reason is that California's capital and the country's can quickly be increased in the same proportion by drawing on the world's supply of savings.

Furthermore, analogies from a single plant or industry to the workings of the economy as a whole are misleading. Increasing the employment of low-productivity workers does not require squeezing them in everywhere. They may go to some industries and not to others; some of the latter may actually lose capacity, and some of the former may not have existed before. The market works in devious ways. Thus the evidence and these commonsense reflections indicate that it does not take much of a reduction in the per-worker cost to employers to induce them to create substantial numbers of new jobs.

Other objections to subsidizing employment are that doing so would raise pay but not employment, and the opposite: that it would increase employment but not pay. The former objection holds that labor unions will seize upon the wage subsidies to raise employees' pay at once, or that firms will feel bound to do that whether or not they face unions. Either way, the subsidies will fail to reduce labor costs even temporarily, and so the stimulus to employment will be nipped in the bud. However, these arguments are inspired by thinking about a proportional *tax rate* on payrolls.[4] They do not apply to an employment subsidy, especially a graduated one that tapers off as the hourly labor cost increases. An employment subsidy, even a fixed one, does not constitute a direct inducement for a rational firm to raise its employees' pay (at the initially given level of the workforce and of the unemployment rate); the subsidies, in reducing labor costs, induce firms to *hire* more. (The end result *is* an upward pull on pay rates, as increased hiring drives down the general unemployment rate, but this is an effect of the success of the subsidy in stimulating hiring, which is precisely the proposition that the objectors deny.)

The latter objection is that the low-wage subsidy may leave the pay of the low-wage worker no higher than it was before. This is odd. If buyers of a computer were given a subsidy, we would expect that the resulting increase in the price buyers could afford to pay would pull up the price received by computer producers, since, at a higher output rate, they would need a higher price to cover the increased unit cost. Similarly, if employers were offered a fixed subsidy per employee, the increased demand for workers would raise the wage received by the workers, since, with employment increased, a higher wage would be required to maintain employee performance and loyalty.

In this discussion of the effect on pay I have abstracted from the plan's graduation of the employment subsidy—as if the subsidy were a flat $3 an hour rather than tapering off. As a consequence of that graduation, the subsidy plan has an impact on the employers' best incentive wage at the *initial* level of employment. The wage that employers set strikes a balance between wage costs and employee performance. The advent of the subsidy with its graduated aspect upsets that balance, making it worthwhile to employers to lower the wage a little in order to gain a higher subsidy.

Clearly this additional wrinkle has no effect on the workers at the *lowest* wage for which an employment subsidy is offered, since lowering their wage would actually disqualify them from any subsidy (or run afoul of minimum wage statues, whichever is the binding factor).

What is the ultimate effect of this complication up the scale? Theoretical work I have done in collaboration with Hian Teck Hoon yields, on some reasonable restrictions embodied by the illustrative plan in Chapter 8, an unambiguous result: the downward effect of graduation on the wage is weaker than the upward pull on pay of the subsidy itself. No worker can suffer a paradoxical decline in pay as a result of the government's supplementing the revenue generated by low-wage employees.[5]

The Perversity Objections

There can be no more poignant commentary on a policy proposal than the objection that it would militate against the very progress it was intended to promote. Foremost among the perversity objections is the contention that low-wage subsidies would doom the disadvantaged to an eternity of dead-end jobs, employment offering little job satisfaction and no prospect for integration into the mainstream of society. Since the subsidies would narrow wage differentials between low-wage and middle-wage jobs, the argument goes, beyond some point they would shrink the return to additional education. The subsidies would thus sap the incentive of low-wage workers to acquire the general knowledge—to invest in the human capital—needed to qualify for higher rungs on the career ladder.

This argument plays on the impression that the natural course of wage differentials is toward equality as more and more workers attain higher education. Equality will be achieved once everyone has an MBA—the American dream. The fear is that an artificial compression of wage differentials through the injection of low-wage employment subsidies would throw a monkey wrench into that process. It would trade off the mansion of equality in the future for a halfway house in the present. But there was no such trend toward shrinking wage inequality, not under the nation's laissez-faire economic policy and not under the interventionist policies in the second half of this century.

A better-grounded view, put somewhat oversimply, is that the wage differential between skilled and unskilled work is a matter of the differential in productivity, and education cannot put a big dent in it, let alone demolish it. (The size of the wage differential determines the number of workers who find it worthwhile to get an education equipping them to master the training for the skilled work; the number educated has little feedback effect onto the size of the wage differential.) Productivity differentials tend to stabilize after a structural shift. The low-wage subsidies would thus tend to make wage differentials forever narrower than they would otherwise be—regardless of their future fluctuations.

Also, the argument gives the impression that America has always had a great chasm between skilled and unskilled wage rates, and that it is this outsize difference that has prompted the expansion of education. So shrinking the wage gap through low-wage subsidies appears as a terrifying leap into the unknown, a move that might discourage education and the whole panoply of things people do to improve themselves. But the fact is that wage differentials have widened enormously since the late 1970s. The proposed low-wage subsidies would not narrow pay differentials much beyond where they were before they were widened by the great wage decompression of the past two decades. So the proposal is more nearly a leap back into the familiar past than into the unknown.

Furthermore, recent evidence does not suggest that wage differentials are a powerful influence on decisions about education. Between 1960 and 1973, when wage differentials were shrinking, the fraction of the young labor force who were high school dropouts shrank by 47 percent; between 1979 and 1993 this fraction fell only 25 percent, despite the greater payoff to moving up the wage ladder that existed in this later period. Similarly, the fraction made up of college graduates rose by one-half in the first period; in the second period it rose by one-half again. Apparently this process is driven by more than one factor, not just wage differentials. It is known, for example, that increases in the schooling of parents or relatives increases the likelihood that the children of those parents will graduate from high school or college.

Moreover, it should not be taken for granted that the low-wage subsidies would tend to retard the upward trend in educational attainment by the less advantaged. These subsidies would help reorient young people toward the rewards of work in the legitimate business sector. The increase in wage rates in the lower part of the distribution would make it worthwhile for disadvantaged youth to investigate and evaluate the new opportunities. A young worker who is drawn into a low-productivity job by the decent pay resulting from the subsidies—instead of unemployment or crime or incarceration—is apt, having gone that far, to be more willing on that account to obtain the additional education necessary to move to a higher rung on the ladder. Thus, more attractive wage rates may do more to enlist the energies and commitment of disadvantaged workers than the narrowing of the percentage differentials will do to reduce those energies and commitment. Once the bourgeois repast is sweetened and made more widely available, more people will respond with bourgeois behavior.

Finally, there is a fundamental flaw in the argument. The argument supposes that the wage differentials generated by the free market are the *right* wage differentials for people to use in calculating the length and course of education to acquire; the low-wage subsidies, in narrowing the wage differentials used in such decisions, would distort those decisions, causing education to be cut short and slanted away from the general knowledge needed for learning the higher skills. But the truth is that the free-market wage rates provide a *wrong* wage differential for educational decisions, since these wages reflect employment decisions by firms that do not take into account the benefit to the rest of society from employing each additional low-wage worker. The free market, in undervaluing unskilled work, *overvalues* the economic gain from additional education for the purpose of qualifying for high-skilled work.

To counter that one would have to say that having young

people continue in school in response to pay in low-wage jobs is just as useful to society as drawing those young people into entry-level jobs through low-wage subsidies. In some cases, that may be so. A job and a year of schooling may be equally effective in keeping a young person away from crime. It would be unrealistic, though, to suppose that low-wage subsidies would draw new recruits to entry-level jobs solely from the student body. Most of the increased jobs would be filled by the unemployed and older persons out of the labor force, few by young persons who would otherwise have enrolled in further schooling.

Jeopardy Objections

These are the objections that the adoption of the new reform is likely to endanger an earlier, more precious accomplishment. Not unexpectedly, there is a jeopardy objection to low-wage subsidies from the right and another from the left.

The objection from the right contends that it is only the citizenry's long-held insistence on leaving people's economic rewards to the marketplace that has spared the country from class warfare. And in doing so it has made available to low-wage workers some material advantages found in very few other countries. Once a system as extensive as low-wage subsidies is introduced, the argument goes, there will be temptations to differentiate them according to industry, family status of the worker, and so forth until the tyranny of majority rule has wrenched the economy into something quite unfair and by a process that could be quite ugly. Politics would loom as a more important determinant of a person's success or failure than his or her own efforts and strategies. It has to be admitted that such an outcome, if it came to pass, would make the proponents of the subsidies wish they had never advanced the idea.

Perhaps the observation that will best allay anxiety on this score is that the federal income tax has not been nearly as riddled with political calculation of votes as might have been imagined; and in fact a strong countermovement toward eliminating most of the exemptions and deductions is a major part of the "tax revolution" of recent years. Having learned how difficult that tax-reform process was, however, we are much less likely to load special treatment of this or that group into the system of employment subsidies.

Conservatives might argue that low-wage subsidies would radically extend government's reach into people's lives. They prefer a smaller government, because they want people to take more responsibility for their lives. But the low-wage subsidy fosters that objective by enabling less advantaged workers to become more economically self-sufficient. It goes further by assisting only those who are willing and eager to work. It thus makes a clear distinction between the moral claims of those who are contributing members of society and those who are not. Unlike those who would dispense welfare willy-nilly to anyone whose income falls below a certain level, I believe that the only genuine entitlement is a reward of self-support and integration for those willing to fulfill a social contract with their fellow citizens by working and earning.

The objection from the left is that low-wage subsidies would represent a use of public tax money to boost the pay of those with low wage rates, some of whom are not poor at all, when possibly that money could have gone instead to widen welfare benefits or raise existing ones in the interest of the extremely poor and the destitute, many of whom are unable to work. A turn toward low-wage employment subsidies as the main thrust of social policy would represent a large risk to the Fabian goal of equality of income. The tension with equalitarianism would be particularly acute where employment subsidies go to low-wage employees who, through inheritance or marriage, are financially independent.

This objection seems not to have come to grips with what is at stake. It is one thing for the state to leave responsibility for the severely handicapped, say, with their parents in cases where the family is rich. (At least a case for such a means test could be made.) It would be quite another if, say, low-wage men or women who married someone earning a seven-figure income had to forfeit the stimulus provided by the state to their employment and thus their inclusion in the economy, their personal growth, and their sense of autonomy. Inequalities are not meaningless or inconsequential. But in a society dedicated to broad opportunity for human liberation and development, equality often has to take a back seat.

The failing of the argument putting equality before everything else is that it makes no distinction between the claims of those who contribute to society and those who, for whatever reason, do not. The rights that persons have in relation to others and the responsibilities they have to others emerge from their transactions with one another. Meeting the claims of those who contribute nothing must not be put ahead of providing increased rewards to persons for increased contribution in return. This is especially so when the added contribution—in budgetary savings and in the surplus going to others from the added collaboration—would more or less cover the proposed rewards. Now, after the long decline of earning power among the disadvantaged, and with our cities witness to an apocalypse of crime and drugs, it is particularly important that our society recognize not just in its rhetoric but in its reward system the social worth of employment as a means to integration into economic life, to self-development, and to self-support.

Epilogue

The early settlers came to the American continent for "the acquisition & free possession of property," as Thomas Jefferson put it.[1] They had no collective purpose for which they sought state support. Establishing a national religion or equalizing incomes or fostering family formation was not on their agenda. They looked to the state only to protect what they saw to be their individual rights.

The Declaration of Independence cited "certain inalienable rights"—among them "life, liberty and the pursuit of happiness." The last of these can only have meant the quest for self-realization and personal development through a career and the other roles and responsibilities that it opens up. Wide private-property rights—the right to sell one's services and to buy and sell property—were understood to derive from the three prior rights.[2] To be enslaved was a clear violation of one's rights.[3]

The signers envisioned a government limited to protecting and promoting citizens' economic opportunity and, so that they would have a democratic voice in how to do that, their political liberty. Jefferson and many of the others had immersed themselves in the Scottish Enlightenment, sifting through the ideas of Ferguson, Hutcheson, Hume, and Smith.[4] Unquestionably the signers' view on the functions of government was the classical liberalism of the Scots. These functions went well beyond Lassalle's night watchman or Carlisle's constable. One function was lawmaking and law enforcement to defend individual rights, of course. National defense was another. But, by the same logic, there was another function, as Adam Smith, summarizing the economic thought of the time, emphasized:

> Thirdly, [the state has] the duty of erecting and maintaining certain public works and certain public institutions, which it can never be for the interest of any individual, or small number of individuals, to erect and maintain; because the profit could never repay the expense to any individual or small number of individuals, though it may frequently do much more than repay it to a great society.[5]

Where additional investment beyond what the market did would bring benefit exceeding cost, state subsidy or direct government provision was justified. Elementary education and religious instruction were discussed at numbing length, as well as "good roads, bridges, navigable canals, harbors, &c." (Smith advocated local-government subsidies to elementary education.) In short, the public sector was to serve economic development—to expand opportunity. Smith did not expect each segment of the citizenry necessarily to repay in user fees the state outlay on its behalf. "The expense . . . for education . . . is . . . no doubt beneficial to the whole society and may therefore, without injustice, be defrayed by the general contribution of the whole society."[6] He saw "equal propriety" in relying on fees, however; a free ride for the upper class would be a bad precedent.[7]

The nation was not being built on selfishness. In the Scots' thinking, humankind was endowed with a moral sense as much as an aesthetic sense; the differences in the choices societies make are to be explained by the differences in their circumstances, Jefferson suggested. The observation of benevolent acts, others' or one's own, was a source of pleasure, and the honor or shame earned by acting well or badly was an incentive to be virtuous. The benevolent societies of the nineteenth century flowed from this spirit. It was hoped the government would be filled with "virtuous" citizens bent on doing their "duty." Yet the force of morality between persons distant from one another was held to be weak.

Popular government, owing to the weakness of morality, was exposed to a moral hazard—the temptation for the legislators arising from special-interest groups.[8] They cannot be expected to resist government benefits paid for by the rest of the country, and legislators cannot be expected to refuse them. If, to buy voter support or campaign contributions, legislators are free to enact special-interest legislation—pork-barrel expenditures, transfers, and tax breaks—and to coerce industry and labor to bear the cost, opportunity and development are bound to suffer.[9] Unchecked public handouts would confront entrepreneurs with overtaxation, overregulation, costly competition for their share of the pork barrel, and uncertainty over what new burdens might strike—with deadening consequences for enterprise and productivity.

The framers of the Constitution struggled with the problem and came up with the system of checks and balances. An act of Congress could be brought by its opponents before the Judiciary for a ruling on its constitutionality. In Madison's words:

> Ambition must be made to counteract ambition. The interest of the man must be connected with the constitutional rights of the place. It may be a reflection on human nature that such devices are necessary . . . If men were angels, no government would be necessary.

Legislatures could not be allowed to judge their own acts:

> No man is allowed to be a judge in his own cause, because his interest would certainly bias his judgment, and, not improbably, corrupt his integrity. With equal, nay with greater reason, a body of men are unfit to be both judges and parties at the same time.

When politicians strayed from their duty to opportunity and development, constitutional supremacy would check them.[10]

It didn't work, though. The country has drifted far from the founding vision. This change is often gauged by the increased taxation over this century. The increase in the tax take has been quite large, of course. More than one-third of the net national product is now swept up by the public sector—22 percent collected by the federal government and about 12 percent by state and local governments.[11] The fraction was only about one-sixth in the early 1930s and far smaller before World War I. The tax take tells us little by itself, though. If these tax revenues were being used primarily to create economic opportunities for workers and investors—if they were going mainly for purposes such as investments in public infrastructure, subsidies to private research and development and for basic science in the public sector, development of backward areas, high-quality primary and secondary education, public safety, and national defense, to give familiar examples—it would be hard to agree that the politicians had circumvented the founders' vision.

The shift in the character of the public sector has been of far greater significance than the change in its size. There has been a stunning change in the nature of public-sector outlays from purchases of public goods and subsidies to private productive activity to the provision of *transfers*. The term denotes payments to persons for having certain attributes, unlike subsidies, which are payments for *doing* a specified thing, such as working. These transfer payments, leaving aside the interest on government debt, are mainly outlays under the entitlement programs for retirees, the destitute, the disabled, veterans, the unemployed, single mothers, and so on. Relating these outlays to, say, wage and salary disbursements, we find that transfer payments equaled nearly 30 percent of earnings in recent years. In 1960 the figure was only 10½ percent.[12] In 1929 it was 3 percent. It was negligible from the inception of the republic until the end of World War I.[13] (In addition, citizens in previous decades awarded themselves government benefits and tax reductions at the expense of the present working-age population—another intergenerational transfer—and the annual interest on the resulting public debt is now considerable.)

This shift in the role of the government has become explicit in the rhetoric of politicians. Classical liberalism is challenged from both the left and the right. Where classical liberalism championed opportunity and development, the left substitutes the new affect-words *equality* and *security*. In this view the purpose of the welfare state is to remove as much as practicable the inequalities and insecurities produced by the capitalist economy. There is no appreciation that enterprise thrives on the outsize inequalities at the top of the distribution; and, most pertinent here, no appreciation that when measures add to labor costs (by dampening the incentives of the less productive to work and perform or by increasing nonlabor costs such as payroll taxes) employability is damaged.

For *equality* and *security* the right substitutes *family* and *children*. The function of government in this view is not to widen and improve private opportunities but to promote a particular social agenda, namely an improvement in the terms available to families and an increase in family formation and stability. There is no appreciation that widening the opportunity for self-supporting employment and improving wage and employment prospects throughout the lower half of the distribution would lead naturally to these ends and others.

The system of subsidies to private employers of low-wage workers for which I have argued in this book fits the founders' conception of our government. The government has a duty, as Smith might have put it, to foster the employment and self-support of the less productive, since it could not be in the interest of any individuals or local communities to do it on the needed scale but it would repay everyone's expense when the costs were spread over the whole society. The social benefits beyond the gain to the low earners themselves—the external benefits—would be enormous. By empowering those with relatively low earning power to be self-supporting and exercise the usual responsibilities, and by drawing into the capitalist mainstream millions of less productive persons who are now depending on welfare, workfare, begging, hustling, and crime, the employment subsidy plan would improve the quality of life for everyone else.

Employment subsidies fit well with the classical tradition seen from another angle. In the Enlightenment view, people have rights. The right to the pursuit of happiness surely means the right to the opportunity to work in society and, through that employment, to be self-supporting, to develop one's capacities, and to assume the responsibilities that are basic for most people—participating in one's community, sustaining relationships with a partner and friends, raising children. If Enlightenment thinkers such as Francis Hutcheson thought it was a violation of one's rights to be enslaved, since it would mean a loss of moral autonomy over a range of one's actions, what would they have thought of a social system in which wage earning is not forbidden to welfare clients but (since their working is not subsidized like their not working) is penalized by a reduction of benefits?[14] There seems to be a loss of moral autonomy as a result of dependency.

In my arguments I have been careful not to presume that the government will first dismantle the welfare system or the whole panoply of entitlements. Let capitalism compete with the welfare system by giving it for the first time since the 1920s a level playing field. Let employment subsidies have at least some small fraction of the vast sum spent on transfer payments. Then, as the employment subsidy succeeds in shrinking welfare's "market share," it will be seen as very nearly self-financing—and any shortfall will certainly be well within the gain that the more advantaged members of society will derive from the full economic collaboration of the disadvantaged.

It would be much better, however, if the initiative described here was merely the first step in the direction of reestablishing and revitalizing the conception of government on which the country was founded. Such a scenario is at least imaginable. With the productive population back at work and able to support themselves and meet basic responsibilities, families will flourish again and children will do well, so there will be no case for injecting the government into decisions on family formation and child raising. Crusades are not wanted in this country, only a limited government conducive to our private pursuits. And with the less productive back on their feet, there will be hope of a reassessment of the government as an insurance company and equalizer of incomes. Removing risks and trying to remove success by soaking the rich might be suitable for a society shell-shocked by inflation, depression, or stagnation, but it seems out of place in a country where there is ample reason to believe that the economic system can continue to deliver prosperity and growth if it is not hamstrung by a dysfunctional economic policy.

We need to return to the founders' thinking. The business of government is fundamentally business, to paraphrase Smith and Coolidge. If we can agree to take the sort of action proposed here to help the less productive help themselves, we may find that we have also helped to restore the founders' conception of a limited and minimal government and helped to preserve the capitalism that the founders provided.

Cost of the Model Wage Subsidy Plan

Hourly wage	Hourly subsidy	Annual wage	Annual subsidy	Number of employees (%)	Number of employees (millions)	Subsidy outlay ($ billions)
$1 or less	$0.00	—	—	0.1%	.061	—
2 to 1.01	0.00	—	—	0.2	.122	—
3 to 2.01	0.00	—	—	0.8	.488	—
4 to 3.01	3.00	$7,000	$6,000	5.9	3.599	$21.594
5 to 4.01	2.29	9,000	4,580	10.4	6.344	29.056
6 to 5.01	1.65	11,000	3,300	9.4	5.734	18.922
7 to 6.01	1.12	13,000	2,240	9.6	5.856	13.117
8 to 7.01	0.71	15,000	1,420	9.1	5.551	7.882
9 to 8.01	0.43	17,000	860	7.0	4.270	3.672
10 to 9.01	0.24	19,000	480	8.1	4.941	2.372
11 to 10.01	0.13	21,000	260	4.2	2.562	0.666
12 to 11.01	0.06	23,000	120	5.3	3.233	0.388
13 to 12.01	0.00	25,000	0	4.6	2.806	0
14 to 13.01	0.00	27,000	0	3.4	2.074	0
15 to 14.01	0.00	29,000	0	3.7	2.257	0
20 to 15.01	0.00	35,000	0	10.4	6.344	0
25 to 20.01	0.00	45,000	0	4.3	2.623	0
More than 25	0.00	—	0	3.5	2.135	0
Total				100.0	61.000	$97.669

Sources: Percentage distribution from the Current Population Survey, March 1990. Number of employees from U.S. Census 1990. Table covers full-time employees in the private sector (full-time employees taken to work 2,000 hours per year).

Notes

Prologue

1. On the wealth of advantages that rural times offered, especially for children and young people entering working age, see William McNeill, "The Disruption of Traditional Forms of Nurture," prepared for the workshop "Capitalism, Socialism and Dictatorship," Luxembourg Institute for European and International Studies, July 12–13, 1996. McNeill comments that the 1920 census was the first to record more Americans living in towns and cities than rural inhabitants in villages and the countryside.

2. From 1870, and no doubt for decades before that, until World War I, the average hourly wage of unskilled urban workers in the United States was more than twice that in Germany and nearly twice that in Britain. (Here and throughout this book the wage refers to the real wage—pay in terms of its purchasing power over consumer goods.) See Jeffrey Williamson, "Globalization, Convergence and History," *Journal of Economic History* 56, June 1996, 277–306.

3. Alexis de Tocqueville, *Democracy in America,* ed. Phillips Bradley, trans. Henry Reeve, New York, Knopf, 1945, Vintage Books ed. 1954.

4. Data from Chinhui Juhn and Kevin M. Murphy, "Inequality in Labor Market Outcomes: Contrasting the 1980s with Earlier Decades," in *Economic Policy Review* 1, January 1995, 27, and from U.S. Bureau of Labor Statistics, Current Population Survey

5. OECD, *National Income Accounts,* 1994, Paris. All dollar magnitudes amounts in this book are given in real terms—that is, they are adjusted for inflation. Social assistance outlays per member of the labor force, deflated by the consumer price index and expressed in 1993 dollars, went from $1,450 in 1974 to $2,100 in 1993.

6. Juhn and Murphy, "Inequality in Labor Market Outcomes."

1. Why Work?

1. The allusion is to John Coleman, *Blue-Collar Journal: A College President's Sabbatical,* Philadelphia, 1974. Coleman, the president of Haverford

177

College, used his sabbatical to work on a garbage truck and operate a dishwasher.

2. Thorstein Veblen, *The Theory of the Leisure Class* (1899), and *The Instinct of Workmanship and the State of the Industrial Arts* (1914). The work on instincts influencing Veblen was William James, *Principles of Psychology* (1891).

3. John Dewey, *Human Nature and Conduct* (1922). Some other social philosophers saw Veblen's impression that capitalists had removed job satisfaction from the available work as showing that there are no instincts, that human nature is only what we are accustomed to seeing. The notion of instincts went into decline. Socialist theorists concluded that communist economies would be able to produce a New Man adapted to that system.

4. Alfred Marshall, *Principles of Economics,* London, Macmillan, 8th ed., 1920, p. 1.

5. My memory is that the newspaper story appeared in the *International Herald Tribune* in the 1980s, but searches have not turned it up. Two other authors who have commented in a similar vein on the healthy effect of a work routine are the French sociologist Pierre Bourdieu and the American sociologist William Julius Wilson.

6. This explanation would seem more persuasive if wage earners showed signs of saving more rather than less. It may be, however, that the decline of private saving over the past few decades is the result of savers' expectation that the welfare state will take care of their medical and other basic needs in old age.

7. Youssef M. Ibrahim, "Europe's Muslim Population: Frustrated, Poor, Divided," *New York Times,* May 5, 1995, pp. 1, 12.

2. America's Second-Class Workers

1. It is a puzzle why physical limitations are so often neglected in discussions of differences in earnings, even though direct observation often suggests they are quite important. One of the morning paper's human interest stories tells of the 43 wrappers, most Latin American women, at a Chinese gourmet shop in Houston. One of them, Paula Villalta, is able to turn out more than 6,000 egg rolls in a typical shift. ("I really concentrate on the egg roll," she explained.) A handful of the others approach her output but can never match it. ("We can't keep up," said one of them. "We try to do it, but we end up exhausted.") The necessary abilities appear to vary widely at the low end as well. Four out of five who try out for the job do not make it. The slowest among the wrappers make about $6.50 an hour while Ms. Villalta earns $9 an hour. *Wall Street Journal,* December 7, 1995, p. 1.

2. Yet some evidence suggests that such bias or prejudice has hardly any

direct effect on earnings after its indirect effects on skills and experience are accounted for. A recent study finds that race has little or no power to explain the differences in wages of recent high school graduates once account is taken of the difference in their scores in a senior year test. Derek A. Neal and William R. Johnson, "The Role of Premarket Factors in Black-White Wage Differences," National Bureau of Economic Research Working Paper 5124, May 1995.

3. Positional goods were introduced into discussions of well-being in Fred Hirsch, *Social Limits to Growth*, Cambridge, Mass., Harvard University Press, 1976.

4. The importance to a person of not being left out of the experience of others having higher incomes is developed in Amartya Sen, *Inequality Reexamined*, Cambridge, Mass., Harvard University Press and Russell Sage Foundation, 1992.

5. U.S. Commerce Department, *Census of Population and Housing 1990* (public use micro-sample data).

6. It is true that the data examined here greatly *understate* the relative earnings of the disadvantaged. Every year there are a great many young workers who have very low earnings but only temporarily—workers starting their careers in entry-level jobs and workers who are down on their luck. A 1992 study showed that 63 percent of minimum-wage workers earn higher wages within a year, with the increases averaging 20 percent. *Industrial Relations and Labor Review,* Washington, U.S. Department of Labor, 1992. These biases in the data are less and less serious higher up the distribution, there being no bias at all at the median. In other respects, however, the relative earnings figures *overstate* the relative position of the more disadvantaged. First, the reported distribution of earnings omits those unemployed the whole of the year. Second, the earnings data necessarily omit those persons among the more disadvantaged who are jobless for other reasons: those who become "discouraged workers" and depend on welfare or resort to crime. Had these workers persisted in the labor force, they might have pulled down the reported average wage and average annual earnings. Consequently these tendencies of the relative earnings figure to overstate the earnings ability of the more disadvantaged workers may offset the tendencies to understate.

7. While in the United States full-time workers at the tenth percentile were earning about 44 percent of median full-time earnings, the corresponding figure was 59 percent in the United Kingdom and reached about 70 percent in the Netherlands and Sweden. The data are from table 2 of Peter Gottschalk and Mary Joyce, "Is Earnings Inequality Also Rising in Other Industrialized Countries?" Boston College, October 1992.

8. Some reasons for this will be touched on in Chapters 6 and 7, including

unemployment insurance benefits and the cushion provided by various other entitlement benefits—their own or those of a parent, spouse, or partner.

9. *The OECD Jobs Study: Evidence and Explanations,* Part II, Paris, 1994, table 7.A.1, p. 161.

10. Calculated from national data in Edmund S. Phelps and Gylfi Zoega, "The Incidence of Increased Unemployment in the Group of Seven, 1970–1994," unpublished paper, Rome, Confindustria, September 1996.

11. *The OECD Jobs Study: Evidence and Explanations,* Part I, Paris, 1994, table 1.6, p. 14. The data reported in the text refer to 1989.

3. The Decline of Labor

1. Robert A. Margo and T. Aldrich Finegan, "Changes in the Distribution of Wages, 1940–50," National Bureau of Economic Research Working Paper 5389, December 1995. The seminal paper on this unusual period is Claudia Goldin and Robert A. Margo, "The Great Compression," *Quarterly Journal of Economics,* February 1992.

2. Chinhui Juhn and Kevin M. Murphy, "Inequality in Labor Market Outcomes: Contrasting the 1980s with Earlier Decades," *Economic Policy Review* 1, no. 1, January 1995, 27.

3. Peter Gottschalk and Mary Joyce, "Is Earnings Inequality Also Rising in Other Industrialized Countries?" Boston College, October 1992.

4. John Bound and George Johnson, "What Are the Causes of Rising Wage Inequality in the United States?" *Economic Policy Review* 1, no. 1, January 1995, table 1, p. 11.

5. *Handbook of Labor Statistics,* Bureau of Labor Statistics, U.S. Department of Labor, Washington, various issues.

6. Ibid.

7. Edmund S. Phelps and Gylfi Zoega, "The Incidence of Increased Unemployment in the Group of Seven, 1970–1994," unpublished paper, Rome, Confindustria, September 1996.

8. *Statistical Abstract of the United States.* Only a few years ago, when I first began to cite this figure, the number in prison had reached 1.1 million. The prison population has been increasing at roughly 100,000 annually.

9. OECD data show a steeper decline, from 89.3 percent in 1970 down to 75.9 in 1989. *The OECD Jobs Study: Evidence and Explanations,* Part I, Paris, 1994, p. 14.

10. It was, by the way, the American economist Paul H. Douglas who, with a mathematician-colleague named Cobb, first detected this constancy, before he went to war and became a United States senator.

11. David Wessel, "The Outlook: As Workers' Pay Lags, Causes Spur a Debate," *Wall Street Journal,* July 31, 1995, p. 1.

12. The rise of labor's share from the mid-1960s to the mid-1970s was not overlooked in the stock market, where share prices adjusted for inflation were on a steep downward trend over that period. When, by 1983 or so, the market could for the first time see capital's share in a recovery, it celebrated with a recovery that, accounting for inflation, finally set record-breaking levels in 1995.

4. The Damage to Others

1. It is reasonable to conceive a level of disadvantage so low that a further decline is not to be expected—unreasonable to think they will all sink to zero employability. But we do not know where the disadvantaged are on that scale. It could be that the magnification of their average level of disadvantage from generation to generation has further to run before the forces of stabilization will have won. Chapter 6 suggests that import competition with the developing world, though in the narrowest sense not a terribly strong factor, is a force that will get worse before tending to get better.

2. Jacob Mincer, "Investment in U.S. Education and Training," Cambridge, Mass., National Bureau of Economic Research, August 1994, table 1. The basic data are in U.S. Department of Education, National Center for Education Statistics, *The Condition of Education,* Washington, 1992.

3. Gilles Saint-Paul, "Unemployment, Wage Rigidity and the Returns to Education," *European Economic Review* 38, September 1994, 535–543.

4. The basic idea here—that it is rational, though not ideal, for an imperfectly informed employer to use applicants' membership in this or that group as proxies for attributes that are expensive or impossible to measure—goes under the heading of statistical discrimination. See Edmund S. Phelps, "The Statistical Theory of Racism and Sexism," *American Economic Review* 62, December 1972, rpt. in Alice Amsden, ed., *The Economics of Women and Work,* Penguin, 1979; and Richard Posner, ed., *Law and Economics,* Cheltenham, Elgar, 1996. See also Kenneth J. Arrow, "The Theory of Discrimination," in *Discrimination in Labor Markets,* ed. Orley Ashenfelter and Albert Rees, Princeton, Princeton University Press, 1973, and Dennis J. Aigner and Glen G. Cain, "Statistical Theories of Discrimination in Labor Markets," *Industrial and Labor Relations Review* 30, January 1977, 175–187.

5. William Julius Wilson, *The Truly Disadvantaged,* Chicago, University of Chicago Press, 1987.

6. U.S. Department of Justice, [Report on Soaring Teenage Violence], Washington, 1995.

7. The presence of low-skilled workers, in adding to the number of workers who can perform low-skilled work relative to complementary fac-

tors of production such as high-skilled workers, undoubtedly drives down somewhat the wage paid such labor—a necessity to get them all hired. (Employers will pay them per worker only what the *last* worker can generate in additional revenue, a smaller amount if there are more of them.) Yet this decrease in the price of unskilled labor must *increase* the income left over for the other factors of production—say, very skilled labor and land. The rent on land or the wage rate paid to very skilled labor—or both—would have to go up.

8. If the disadvantaged brought skills making them like the high skilled and nearly as productive at everything, they would contribute virtually nothing to the income of the latter. It would just be a case of more of the same, with no gains from exchange. At the other extreme, if the disadvantaged have no necessary skills at all, they again contribute nothing to the others.

9. *Statistical Abstract of the United States: 1991.* Tables on State and Local Government Police Protection and Correction and on the Criminal Justice System.

10. See Thomas Sowell, *The Vision of the Anointed: Self-Congratulation as a Basis for Social Policy,* New York, Basic Books, 1995.

11. Irving Kristol, "The Way We Were," *Wall Street Journal,* July 14, 1995, p. A12.

12. *Statistical Abstract of the United States: 1991.* Table on Crime Rates—Selected Large Cities.

13. The American work was begun in Dorothy Swaine Thomas, *Social Aspects of the Business Cycle,* New York, Dutton, 1925. This and other references may be found in Chapter 4 of my *Inflation Policy and Unemployment Theory,* New York, Norton, 1972.

14. Herbert Stein and Murray Foss, *The Illustrated Guide to the American Economy,* 2nd ed., Washington, American Enterprise Institute Press, 1995, p. 213.

5. Is It Culture?

1. The increased waiting time that anyone who becomes unemployed would expect before landing a job serves to dampen quitting and shirking, thus to raise productivity and to encourage employers to moderate their wages, at least relative to their previously elevated level.

2. On the neoclassical view, the withdrawal of some workers from the labor force could only push the hourly wage up, never down. Even in the modern view, a decline in some employees' loyalty and dedication to their jobs might leave the wage higher in the end (see the next note). The positive effect hinges on the supposition that, as a result of the ensuing contraction

in these workers' employment, those who remain employed will be scarcer than before and therefore command a higher wage. But the size of this positive effect will be negligible if these workers are easily replaced by other sorts of workers or by equipment. Where the labor input of workers pushing on wages is highly substitutable for other inputs, the wage must end up hardly above where it began. The globalization of trade has made this substitutability greater than ever.

3. In contrast, some modern formulations, in their quest for simplicity, exclude the very case highlighted in the text. In these formulations, the slightest deterioration of workforce performance would be disastrously costly; so the employer's least-cost response is to restore job performance to its necessary level through a sufficient pay increase—then slim down the workforce to what can be afforded. Since no deterioration in job performance results, there is no decline in the workers' productivity, hence no fall in the demand for labor. Employment falls only because the going industry wage has been pushed up, raising the price of labor to every firm. Unemployment rises until the wage has subsided back to the initial level of productivity.

4. A. W. Phillips, "The Relation between Unemployment and the Rate of Change of Money Wage Rates in the United Kingdom, 1861–1957," *Economica,* New Series, 25, November 1958. The standard historical series on the unemployment rate (estimated from 1890 until 1939 from decennial census data) is contained in Stanley Lebergott, *Manpower in Economic Growth,* New York, McGraw-Hill, 1964.

5. And this in spite of a rise of public dissaving as measured by government deficits from not quite 1.5 percent to 3 percent over the same period. (Instead of saving the deficit-financed tax cuts and transfers for the sake of their heirs, the public spent most or all of them.)

6. See for example Gertrude Himmelfarb, *The De-Moralization of Society: From Victorian Values to Modern Values,* New York, Basic Books, 1995.

7. This observation and its contrast with the next generation is made in Alan Ehrenhalt, *The Lost City: Discovering the Forgotten Virtues of Community in the Chicago of the 1950s,* New York, Basic Books, 1996.

8. This fact was brought up in a televised debate among Nicholas Leman, Mickey Kaus, and James Taranto, C-SPAN, May 1994.

9. These figures are cited in Barry Bluestone, "Economic Inequality and the Micro-Structuralist Debate," in Robert Heilbroner and Charles Whalen, eds., *Economics for the Twenty-First Century,* Armonk, N.Y., M. E. Sharp, 1996.

10. The two leading black economists on the subject of the black experience in this country, Glenn Lowry and Thomas Sowell, appear to represent a movement against emphasis on victimization.

11. Evidence for this effect is found in Yoram Ben-Porath, "Production of Human Capital and the Life-Cycle of Earnings," *Journal of Political Economy*, August 1967, and Gary Becker, *Human Capital*, 2nd ed., Chicago, University of Chicago Press, 1975.

12. Peter Davis, *If You Came This Way*, New York, Wiley, 1996.

13. Richard Rorty, "Color-Blind in the Marketplace" (review of Dinesh D'Souza, *The End of Racism*), *New York Times Book Review*, September 24, 1995, p. 9.

14. The recent series of books on the transition to capitalism include Jeffrey Sachs, *Poland's Jump to the Market Economy*, Cambridge, Mass., MIT Press, 1993; Roman Frydman and Andrzej Rapaczynski, *Privatization in Eastern Europe: Is the State Withering Away?* London, Central European University Press, 1994; and Maxim Boycko, Andrei Shleifer, and Robert Vishny, *Privatizing Russia*, Cambridge, Mass., Harvard University Press, 1995.

15. Rorty, "Color-Blind in the Marketplace."

6. Economic Sources

1. Casey B. Mulligan and Xavier Sala-i-Martin, "A Labour-Income-Based Measure of the Value of Human Capital: An Application to the United States," Discussion Paper no. 1146, Centre for Economic Policy Research, March 1995.

2. See Nuala Beck, *Shifting Gears: Thriving in the New Economy*, New York, HarperCollins, 1995.

3. Richard R. Nelson and Edmund S. Phelps, "Investment in Humans, Technological Diffusion and Economic Growth," *American Economic Review* 56, May 1966.

4. Alternatively these poorly prepared workers are hired anyway and given skimpy training, with the result that they are actually less productive than they would have been under the old technology and they are paid less accordingly—the case considered in the previous section. In this case the *gross* productivity of underprepared workers is reduced by the technological advances.

5. See Ann Bartel and Frank Lichtenberg, "The Comparative Advantage of Educated Workers in Implementing New Technologies," *Review of Economics and Statistics* 69, February 1987.

6. See Jess Benhabib and Mark M. Siegel, "The Role of Human Capital and Political Instability in Economic Development," *Rivista di Politica Economica* 11, November 1992; Robert J. Barro and Xavier Sala-i-Martin, "Technological Diffusion, Convergence and Growth," London, Bank of England, March 1995; Darius Palia and Edmund S. Phelps, "The Empirical

Importance of Private Ownership in Economic Growth," paper presented at the Villa Mondragone International Seminar, University of Rome "Tor Vergata," June 1996.

7. Stephen Nickell, "The Collapse in the Demand for the Unskilled: What Can be Done?" paper presented at a conference of the Russell Sage Foundation, Demand-Side Strategies and Low-Wage Labor Markets, New York, June 1995.

8. See Robert Hall, "Comment: Trade and Jobs in U.S. Manufacturing," *Brookings Papers on Economic Activity,* Spring 1994, 74–77.

9. The beginnings of the trade thesis are hard to trace. Early and strong proponents include Edward Leamer, "Effects of a U.S.-Mexico Free Trade Agreement," National Bureau of Economic Research Working Paper, 1991; Adrian Wood, *North-South Trade, Employment and Inequality: Changing Fortunes in a Skill-Driven World,* Oxford, Clarendon Press, 1994; George J. Borjas and Valerie Ramey, "Time-Series Evidence on the Sources of Trends in Wage Inequality," *American Economic Review* 84, May 1994, 10–16.

10. Jeffrey D. Sachs and Howard J. Shatz, "Trade and Jobs in U.S. Manufacturing," *Brookings Panel on Economic Activity,* Spring 1994, 1–84, estimates that in the period 1978–1990, during which trade with developing countries expanded considerably, a loss of 1.2 million jobs in manufacturing, or about two-fifths of the total loss over the period, could be attributed to the rise in imports from the developing countries. An analysis of the American data with more of a focus on wages is Robert Z. Lawrence and Matthew J. Slaughter, "Trade and U.S. Wages: Giant Sucking Sound or Small Hiccup?" *Brookings Panel on Economic Activity: Microeconomics* 2, Fall 1993, 161–210.

11. Sachs and Shatz, "Trade and Jobs in U.S. Manufacturing."

12. Jagdish Bhagwati and Vivek Dehejia, "Free Trade and Wages of the Unskilled: Is Marx Striking Again?" paper presented at the Conference on the Influence of Trade on U.S. Wages, American Enterprise Institute, September 1993.

13. Paul R. Krugman and Robert Z. Lawrence, "Trade, Jobs and Wages," *Science,* April 1994, 44–49.

14. Lawrence and Slaughter, "Trade and U.S. Wages."

15. Alan B. Krueger, "Labor Market Shifts and the Price Puzzle Revisited," paper presented at a conference in honor of Assar Lindbeck, Unemployment and Wage Dispersion: Is There a Tradeoff? Stockholm, June 16–18, 1995.

16. It is also said that, contrary to what the trade thesis suggests, unskilled unemployment has been *falling* as a ratio to skilled unemployment in several European countries (though that would not be my reading of the

data). See Steven Nickell and Brian Bell, "The Collapse in Demand for the Unskilled and Unemployment across the OECD," *Oxford Review of Economic Policy* 11, Spring 1995, 40–62.

17. An additional point is that the mere anticipation by domestic producers of a shrinking market share may translate into less capacity expansion and maintenance and thus ultimately less hiring in manufacturing than is accounted for by existing studies.

18. Much of this paragraph is supported in Edmund S. Phelps and Gylfi Zoega, "The Incidence of Increased Unemployment in the Group of Seven, 1970–1994," unpublished paper, Rome, Confindustria, September 1996.

19. Just how the firm responds to this development with regard to the wages it will pay preexisting employees is something we need not enter into. But it is clear that the firm will be unwilling to hire new employees, as additions to the workforce or as replacements when existing employees leave, at the previous wage level, since the investment outlay in initial training is unchanged but the stream of output expected from the new employee must be discounted by a higher interest rate.

7. The Role of the Welfare System

1. If we had to look to the public spirit and cooperation of private citizens for our lighthouses, standing army, language and math instruction, inoculation programs, and so forth, there would tend to be a considerable undersupply of these goods which, up to a point, are in the general interest; an undersupply created as many beneficiaries try to pass on to others the burden of supplying them. And insofar as the private sector did muster supplies of some of these goods, there would be a tendency for underconsumption of them—the problem being that the private suppliers would need to charge to recoup their costs, causing users to consume them more sparingly or infrequently, while the government could afford to reduce the price to an ideal level, often zero, through relatively low tax rates on a broad base of households' total spending or earning. (In Britain lighthouses *are* private. An explanation is that the payment of the lighthouse dues can be made part of the charges for using the port.)

2. These are estimates by the National Science Foundation, as reported by Peter Passell in the *New York Times*, November 9, 1995, p. D2.

3. Interview with Secretary of Labor Robert Reich, "Morning Edition," National Public Radio, April 11, 1995.

4. The premise here was the Keynesian faith that an increase in any or all government expenditures (or subsidies), like an increase in any private consumption or investment expenditure, would add something on balance (after allowing for any "crowding out") to total expenditure. This boost to "effective demand," as it was called, induced employers to step up employment in

order to produce more output. The elevation of employment was sustained, according to the theory, because producers remained slow to hike their prices (and money wages) in response to the increased money demand for their output.

5. Talk by Daniel Yankelovich to the Groupe franco-américain d'observation réciproque, Fondation nationale des sciences politiques/Société Tocqueville, Paris, June 1985.

6. Some of the leading econometric investigations of the influences on the unemployment rate are in works by Richard Layard, Steven Nickell, Andrew Newell, James Symons, Charles Bean, David Coe, Patrick Minford, Dennis Snower, and Albert Ando. There is also my research in collaboration with Gylfi Zoega, cited earlier. To date, public expenditure does not appear to be a very successful explanatory variable.

7. Luigi Bonatti, "The Firms' Investment and the Unskilled Workers' Search Activity in a Dynamic Model of a Dual Economy," Trento, University of Trento, July 1995.

8. *Bureaucrats in Business,* Washington, World Bank, 1995.

9. Seymour Martin Lipset, "Beyond 1984: The Future of American Politics," in Jesse R. Pitts and Olivier Zunz, eds., *Tocqueville Review* 7, Charlottesville, University of Virginia, 1985/86, p. 167. This paragraph and the previous one have benefited from Lipset's discussion of American values, which draws in turn from his book *The First New Nation.*

10. Edmund S. Phelps and Gylfi Zoega, "The Incidence of Increased Unemployment in the Group of Seven, 1970–1994," unpublished paper, Rome, Confindustria, August 1996.

11. For single or married persons with two or more qualifying children paying taxes on 1995 income, the first dollar of wage earnings and each succeeding dollar brings a credit of 36¢, until at the wage income of $8,600 the credit reaches a cap around $3,110; at the wage income of $11,300 the credit then begins to decrease by 20¢ for each additional dollar earned, hitting zero at the wage income of $26,673. With one child the cap is $2,094 and with no children the cap is $314 in the 1995 tax tables (see Form 1040, pp. 27–31).

12. Amartya Sen, Lecture, Columbia University, October 1972.

13. The question of whether the working population has such "associative duties" to noncontributing fellow nationals while not, for example, to noncontributing foreigners has attracted the interest of some philosophers lately. See for example Samuel Scheffler, "Individual Responsibility in a Global Age," *Social Philosophy and Policy* 12, 219–236.

14. Gylfi Zoega, "A Structural Model of Equilibrium Unemployment: Theory, Evidence and Dynamic Simulations," Ph.D. dissertation, Columbia University, 1993.

15. Phelps and Zoega, "Incidence of Increased Unemployment in the

Group of Seven, 1970–1994," unpublished paper, Rome, Confindustria, August 1996.

16. Charles Murray, *Losing Ground*, New York, Basic Books, 1984.

17. Report by Stephen Moore and Michael Tanner, Cato Institute, Washington, September 1995.

18. An important part of the theoretical reasoning is that the workers' propensities to quit and so forth are driven by the wage as a ratio to their nonwage income, and this nonwage income is not reduced by the payroll tax, only the wage is reduced—hypothetically by the full amount of the drop in the demand wage in the first stage of the analysis.

8. The Market-Based Solution

1. The term wage subsidy is more frequent in the economics literature. But employment subsidy better conveys the idea that it is employment that is being directly encouraged. The resulting expansion of employment can be expected to induce a rise of wage rates at the low end.

2. The hourly wage cost is *before* the addition of the employer-paid part of the payroll tax and *after* subtraction of the employment subsidy. The gross wage is also *before* deduction of the employee-paid part of the payroll tax. (The wedge between the hourly labor cost including tax and the wage net of employment tax is therefore the total employment tax less any employment subsidy.)

3. More accurately, the wage (net of the employee-paid employment tax) that employers can afford to pay an employee is only the employee's private productivity less any employer-paid payroll tax or other employment-related tax and plus any subsidies on such employment.

4. See for example Price V. Fishback and Shawn E. Kantor, "Did Workers Pay for the Passage of Workers' Compensation Laws?" National Bureau of Economic Research Working Paper 4947, December 1994.

5. It could be argued that it is an essential benefit, for if the sole benefit were simply an increase of employment at the same old unsatisfactory pay rates—if the gain were only that people did not have to search or to wait so long when between jobs—there would be an increase in self-support and the sense of self-reliance, but the gulf between the less advantaged and the more advantaged would be only modestly narrowed. For example, if the unemployment rate in a poor neighborhood shrank from 20 percent to 10, that would boost average earnings by just one-eighth.

6. Richard Jackman and Richard Layard, "A Wage-Tax, Worker-Subsidy Policy for Reducing the 'Natural Rate of Unemployment,'" in Wilfred Beckermann, ed., *Wage Rigidity*, Baltimore, Johns Hopkins University Press, 1986, pp. 153–169.

7. I remember being part of a group advising Senator Robert Kennedy, all of whom, from James Tobin to the young Martin Feldstein, were supporters of the scheme. None of us saw the importance of tying such support to work.

8. Hian Teck Hoon and Edmund S. Phelps, "Low-Wage Employment Subsidies in a Labor-Turnover Model of the 'Natural Rate,'" Department of Economics, Columbia University, September 1996.

9. The formula behind this table, devised by Hian Teck Hoon and Lian Leck Hoon, is $s = a \exp\{- b\, v_f^2\}$, where s is the subsidy and v_f is the hourly cost to the firm.

10. There is a small effect of the proportional payroll tax on the required incentive wage. With the payroll tax increased in order to finance the subsidies, the firm will calculate that a small cut of its hourly labor cost will bring a larger benefit in reduced payroll taxes on the employees' pay than it would have before. So the firm will see that the wage required by incentive reasons has been reduced by the increase in the payroll tax rate. The main effect of this complication is that employment will be expanded a little. But if, as the text assumes, employment level has little effect on the affordable wage, wages will still fall as a result of the extra payroll tax in the simple way stated in the text.

9. The Case for the Market-Based Solution

1. Two very limited exceptions to this sweeping description are the statutory minimum wage law and the Earned Income Tax Credit, both to be discussed below.

2. Some notions of *real* justice are involved, though. I argue later that the rest of society will not only derive benefits from reduced crime and so on, the budgetary savings and revenue gains from which are sufficient to finance the subsidy plan. It will also draw satisfaction from acting on its sense of justice in returning to the disadvantaged the additional gain from the intensified collaboration of the disadvantaged in the economy—rather than retaining the resulting increase in its wages and rents (insofar as that income increase can be retained without underfinancing the subsidy program).

3. Public finance economics explains that besides this direct private burden on taxpayers there is a so-called excess burden arising from the weakening of their incentives to save, participate in the labor force, and be good employees. Symmetrically, when the employment of a category of workers is subsidized there is on top of their direct private benefit an excess benefit resulting from their strengthened incentives to save, to work and, when working, be good employees. For the sake of simplicity in the text I take the excess burden to be more or less counterbalanced by the excess benefit. Therefore, since the direct private cost of the subsidies to taxpayers must

equal the direct private benefit to the beneficiaries (mostly the affected workers), I take the total private benefit to be more or less equal to the total private cost.

4. We want the corporate tax rate multiplied by about 10 percent of the added corporate income, which consists of the increase in profits resulting from the expansion of output (since ultimately the employment subsidies are largely passed on to the workers' wages). An exact calculation has not been made.

5. Kenneth J. Arrow, *The Limits of Organization,* New York, Norton, 1974, p. 26. In the passage quoted Arrow adds that "the fact that we cannot mediate all our responsibilities to others through prices . . . makes it essential in the running of society that we have what might be called 'conscience,' a feeling of responsibility for the effects of one's actions on others." Judging from the import of the passage he might better have written "the effects of one's actions *or inaction* on others."

6. Gunnar Eskelund, letter to the editor, *Financial Times,* May 25/26, 1996, p. 8.

7. Arthur M. Okun, *Equality and Efficiency: The Big Tradeoff,* Washington, Brookings Institution, 1975.

8. Friedrich A. Hayek, *The Constitution of Liberty,* Chicago, University of Chicago Press, 1960, pp. 85–102.

9. John Rawls, *A Theory of Justice,* Cambridge, Mass., Harvard University Press, 1971, p. 7.

10. Hayek, p. 101. It is not clear whether Hayek had in mind social support for the weak who were *never* strong and the infirm who were *never* well, since he refers to "certain risks common to all citizens."

11. The exact content of the terms being described may be illustrated by a comparison. The Good Samaritan of the biblical parable cooperates with the wretch he has come upon free of charge. But would he be prepared to do that if he anticipated such encounters every few minutes throughout his business day? In contrast, the *just* Samaritan charges for his time. If by working together he and the other could catch eight fish while it would cost him what he could catch working alone, say five fish, he will charge five for his time. And this regardless of the fact that the other is left with less.

12. H. Steinhaus, "The Problem of Fair Division," *Econometrica* 16, January 1948, 101–104.

13. Ayn Rand, *The Virtue of Selfishness,* New York, New American Library, 1964. Rand does not reflect on whether that arrangement is really cost-effective, thus efficient. Perhaps the "free riders," by paying a small share of the cost (a clear gain to the others), would gain on balance from the resulting incentives toward more frequent bus service.

14. Even if it were feasible to redistribute more and more of the surplus

to the disadvantaged until the advantaged had almost none left, the wage of the disadvantaged would not be pulled up to equality, since, in our stylized view at any rate, the advantaged can do everything the disadvantaged can do and more.

15. Rawls, *A Theory of Justice.*

16. In a hypothetical calculation, Gilles Saint-Paul and I found the gain to be in this surprisingly low neighborhood.

10. The Flaws in Other Approaches

1. A. C. Pigou, *The Theory of Unemployment,* London, Macmillan, 1933, ch. 11. Kaldor's paper, "Wage Subsidies as a Remedy for Unemployment," was read at the annual American meeting of the Econometric Society, New York, December 1935, and published in the *Journal of Political Economy* 44, December 1936.

2. Richard Layard and Richard Jackman, "The Efficiency Case for Long-Run Labour Market Policies," *Economica* 47, August 1980, 331–349; and Richard Jackman and Richard Layard, "A Wage-Tax, Worker-Subsidy Policy for Reducing the 'Natural Rate of Unemployment,'" in Wilfred Beckermann, ed., *Wage Rigidity,* Baltimore, Johns Hopkins University Press, 1986, pp. 153–169.

3. Daniel S. Hammermesh, "Subsidies for Jobs in the Private Sector," in J. Palmer, ed., *Creating Jobs,* Washington, Brookings Institution, 1978; Robert H. Haveman and John L. Palmer, eds., *Jobs for Disadvantaged Workers,* Washington, Brookings Institution, 1982; M. D. Hurd and John Pencaval, "A Utility-Based Analysis of the Wage-Subsidy Program," *Journal of Public Economics* 15, April 1981, 185–201.

4. Dennis J. Snower, "Getting the Benefit out of a Job," *Financial Times,* February 23, 1993. My own papers on employment subsidies include "Economic Justice to the Working Poor through a Wage Subsidy," in Dimitri Papadimitriou, ed., *Aspects of the Distribution of Wealth and Income,* New York, St. Martins, 1994; "Low-Wage Subsidies versus the Welfare State," *American Economic Review* 84, May 1994; "Wage Subsidy Programmes: Alternative Designs," in Guillermo de la Dehesa and Dennis Snower, eds., *Unemployment Policy: Government Options for the Labour Market,* London, Centre for Economic Policy Research, 1996; and with Hian Teck Hoon, "Low-Wage Employment Subsidies in a Labor-Turnover Model of the 'Natural Rate,'" Department of Economics, Columbia University, September 1996.

5. See for example Dale T. Mortensen, "Reducing Supply-Side Disincentives to Job Creation," in *Reducing Unemployment: Current Issues and Policy Options,* Federal Reserve Bank of Kansas City, 1994; Lawrence F.

Katz, "Wage Subsidies for the Disadvantaged," in Richard Freeman and Peter Gottschalk, eds., *Demand-Side Strategies for Low-Wage Labor Markets,* New York, Russell Sage Foundation, 1996; Stephen Nickell and Brian Bell, "Would Cutting Payroll Taxes on the Unskilled have a Significant Impact on Unemployment?" in de la Dehesa and Snower, eds., *Unemployment Policy;* and Christopher A. Pissarides, "The Modeling of Employment Taxes in Labour Market Equilibrium," London School of Economics, May 1995.

6. Possibly the thinking is strategic: once the minimum wage increase is passed and employment among the disadvantaged worsens, the government will finally be pressured to take the *other* steps necessary to boost low-wage employment. It would be better, however, to proceed directly with the subsidies and never mind the minimum wage increase—wages will be pulled up by the market without it.

7. U.S. Department of Labor, unsigned briefing paper, "The Future of Work," April 28, 1994.

8. Peter Robinson, "The Role and Limits of Active Labor Market Policy," paper prepared for the Conference on Unemployment, European University Institute, Florence, April 12–13, 1996.

9. James Heckman, "Assessing Clinton's Program on Job Training, Workfare, and Education in the Workplace," National Bureau of Economic Research Working Paper 4428, August 1993.

10. Gilles Saint-Paul, "Unemployment, Wage Rigidity and the Returns to Education," *European Economic Review* 38, September 1994, 535–543. The available data are not rich enough to permit us to confirm—or reject—the presence of this effect with any confidence.

11. Bennett, *The Book of Virtues,* New York, Simon and Schuster, 1994; Himmelfarb, *The De-Moralization of Society: From Victorian Values to Modern Values*, New York, Basic Books, 1995.

12. The term is used in Christopher Clausen, "The Politics of Gestures," *New Leader* 72, June 5–19, 1995, 13–16.

11. Reply to Objections

1. Albert O. Hirschman, *The Rhetoric of Reaction: Perversity, Futility, Jeopardy,* Cambridge, Mass., Harvard University Press, 1991.

2. Casey B. Mulligan and Xavier Sala-i-Martin, "A Labour-Income-Based Measure of the Value of Human Capital: An Application to the United States," Centre for Economic Policy Research Discussion Paper No.1146, March 1995, pp. 35–36 and table 10, p. 54.

3. Jacob Mincer, *Studies in Human Capital,* Hants, England, Edward Elgar, 1993, p. 386.

4. As noted in Chapter 7, the contractionary effect of using the payroll tax rather than the virtually neutral value-added tax is partially eroded as workers adjust their wealth downward to their lower pay, especially in an open economy such as the American one. (However, many low-wage workers may have declined to accumulate private assets in view of their extensive social wealth, and so will not make this neutralizing adjustment.) Similarly, the employment effect of a cut in the payroll tax rate instead of a cut in the value-added tax is partly dissipated as workers' wealth climbs toward its former relation to pay.

5. Hian Teck Hoon and Edmund S. Phelps, "Low-Wage Employment Subsidies in a Labor-Turnover Model of the 'Natural Rate,'" Department of Economics and Statistics, Columbia University, September 1996.

Epilogue

1. Julian P. Boyd et al., *The Papers of Thomas Jefferson*, 19 vols., Princeton, Princeton University Press, 1950–1974, vol. 1, p. 193.

2. Gary Wills, *Inventing America: Jefferson's Declaration of Independence*, New York, Random House, 1978, pp. 229–239. In the Enlightenment terminology, the right to one's property was an *alienable* right since one could sell the property, divest one's self of it. (But just why all alienable rights have to be derived from inalienable ones is not clear to me.)

3. As Wills details, Jefferson unmistakably saw slavery on the American continent as a violation of rights (though he thought that as a practical matter emancipation would best be done through creation of a separate nation). The thesis that emancipation was a delayed fulfillment of the Declaration and the Constitution is further argued in Harry V. Jaffa, *How to Think about the American Revolution*, Durham, N.C., Carolina Academic Press, 1978.

4. Wills, *Inventing America*, pp. 248–255.

5. Adam Smith, *The Wealth of Nations* (1776), 5th Cannan ed., London, Methuen, 1961, IV, ix, 51.

6. Ibid.

7. Smith believed that wages at the low end tended always to the subsistence level; the government could not tax them down or subsidize them up. So Smith did not recognize any possibility that economic policy could make a permanent difference to the wages of the least productive.

8. I am drawing here on Terry L. Anderson and Peter J. Hill, *The Birth of a Transfer Society*, Stanford, Hoover Institution Press, 1980, pp. 24–27.

9. Free riders will dodge voluntary regulations and suggested tax contributions.

10. James Madison, *The Federalist*, 51, 10.

11. These figures are calculated from 1992 data in *Economic Report of the President,* February 1994, tables B-23 and B-80. The state and local government figure cited here consists only of taxes and thus excludes grants-in-aid received from the federal government.

12. Ibid., February 1994, table B-26. The recent figure is based on 1992.

13. Anderson and Hill, *Birth of a Transfer Society,* ch. 7. Anderson and Hill focus on the government's interventions through industrial regulation, which reduce the rewards to investors and workers, a departure pressured by agrarian radicals, Populists, and later Progressives in the period between 1877 and 1917.

14. Wills, *Inventing America,* ch. 15, pp. 218–228, esp. p. 228.

Index

American experiment, 1
Arrow, K. J., 135
Asian emigrants, 58
Attitudes: effects of, 52–53; cultural influences on, 53–56

Bismarck, O., 46, 91
Blacks, 29, 40–43; American history of, 56–58; thesis of distinctive black culture, 58–59; black leaders, 85–86, 147
Bonatti, L., 86

Capitalism. *See* Free enterprise
Carlisle, T., 168
Children: damage to, 37–38; influence of Depression on, 55, 62; as political base, 171
Civic responsibilities, 1, 54–56, 94, 100, 128
Cohesion, social: access to community life, 1, 2, 5
Collaboration, gain from: 44, 137–143; collaborators as the claimants, 135–137, 166; views on its distribution, 138–140; ballpark estimate, 141
Community life, 1, 12, 14, 21–22. *See also* Civic responsibilities
Coolidge, C., 15, 173
Crime, 2, 4, 43, 45–46
Cultural influences, 51–63
Cultural policy, 51
Culture of poverty, 128
Cycle of poverty, 38

Davis, P., 58
Dependency, 3–4, 95, 99

Depression (Great), 46, 55
Dewey, J., 11
Disadvantage, economic: depth of, 4, 23; sources of, 18; demarcated, 18–22; dependence on welfare, 23; breadth of, 24. *See also* Unemployment of disadvantaged; Labor force of disadvantaged
Discrimination, 60–61; rational, 60; statistical, 61
Drugs, 2, 4, 43

Earned Income Tax Credit, 88; savings from its replacement, 132–135
Earning, role of: material gains from, 13–14; providing for others, 14; source of self-support, 14; and social importance, 15
Education, 30–31, 39–40, 67–70, 87–88, 161–163; proposals, 150–153
Employment subsidies: nature of, 5–6, 105–106; issues, 6, 154–166; alleged ineffectiveness, 157–161; alleged perversity, 161–164; needy jeopardized, 164–166. *See also* Employment subsidy proposal; Hiring subsidies
Employment subsidy proposal: rationale for, 106–107, 124–125; eligible wage rates, 107; abuses, 107–108, 114–115; flat subsidy examined, 107–111; eligible employers, 108; restricted to full-time jobs, 108; the graduated plan, 112–116; illustrative graduated schedule, 114; effect on wages and unemployment, 115–116; effects of interim financing, 117–118; budgetary savings resulting,

195